the pilgrim way
to
santiago
~de~
compostela

cay

FRANCE

santander

CANTABRIA

BILBAO

Biarritz

ebro

Roncesvalles

pamplona

estella

navarra

Burgos

La
RIOJA

Logroño

arga

sta

pisuerga

valladolid

aragon

stile

í   n

150   200   250   km

Spanish Pilgrimage

To Diana

from Jörn

for everything

7 | 1994

The Rough and the Smooth
A Question of Survival
A Pattern of Peoples
Mulu: the Rain Forest
Aborigines of the Amazon Rain Forest: the Yanomani
Worlds Apart
White Horses over France
A Ride Along the Great Wall
Fragile Eden

SPANISH PILGRIMAGE

A CANTER TO ST JAMES

Robin Hanbury-Tenison

HUTCHINSON

London Melbourne Auckland Johannesburg

This edition first published in 1990 by
Hutchinson

Century Hutchinson Ltd
20 Vauxhall Bridge Road, London, SW1V 2SA

Century Hutchinson Australia (Pty) Ltd
20 Alfred Street, Milsons Point, Sydney NSW 2061, Australia

Century Hutchinson New Zealand Ltd
PO Box 40–086, Glenfield, Auckland 10, New Zealand

Century Hutchinson South Africa (Pty) Ltd
PO Box 337, Bergvlei, 2012 South Africa

British Library Cataloguing in Publication Data
Hanbury-Tenison, Robin, 1936–
   Spanish Pilgrimage.
   1. Spain. Navarre. Christian pilgrimages to Santiago de
   Compostela. Routes. Description & travel
   I. Title
   248.463094652

   ISBN 0–09–174322–2

Set in Linotron Sabon by Input Typesetting Ltd, London
Printed and bound in Great Britain by
Butler and Tanner Ltd, Frome, Somerset

The author and publisher wish to thank
the Estate of Dorothy L. Sayers and Penguin Books
Ltd for permission to quote from the translation
of 'The Song of Roland'

For Merlin

Canter. An easy gallop; originally called a Canterbury pace or gallop, from the ambling gait adopted by mounted pilgrims to the shrine of St Thomas à Becket at Canterbury.

Brewer's Dictionary of Phrase and Fable

Canter. One who uses the cant of thieves, etc.; a rogue, vagabond. A talker of professional or religious cant 1652.

Oxford English Dictionary

CONTENTS

The legend of St James, a drawing by Brian Partridge

INTRODUCTION

T he Yeoman Warder saluted as we rode into Her Majesty's Tower of London, and waved us on to the next gate. The crowds viewing this, the most visited site in Britain, parted as we clattered over the cobbles and crossed the drawbridge spanning the moat. A raven flapped off the grass in alarm and croaked crossly at us from a battlement.

Of course, we should have been on white horses – my wife Louella and I – as we went to call on the Governor and pay our 'custom' before setting out on our pilgrimage to the shrine of St James. And we would have been on Thibert and Tiki – our sweet Camargues on whom we had ridden across France five years before – had it not been for a dreadful disease, African Horse Sickness, which had broken out in Spain and made it impossible to think of taking them there.

Instead we were on the small motor-bike we keep in London for use on our infrequent visits. As a further indignity, I was riding pillion behind Louella, since unlike her I do not have a full licence. Nonetheless we had been given permission to ride to the Governor's house, and we did so with as much dignity as we could.

The Governor of the Tower of London (or as he was known in earlier centuries, the Constable or Lieutenant) used to be a person of great importance with considerable patronage at his disposal. He was paid fees by state prisoners, nicely graduated according to rank. Dukes paid £20, earls £15, barons £10 and knights 23s 4d, while gentlemen paid 17s 6d. He was also entitled to fleece everyone who used the Thames deliberately or accidentally. All cattle which fell off London Bridge were his, as were any swans that floated below the bridge, and all flotsam and jetsam. Carts falling into the Tower ditch became his absolute property. From every ship laden with wine from Bordeaux, or elsewhere, 'one flagon from before and another from behind the mast' were his, the selection presumably ensuring a varied cellar. A basketful of oysters, mussels or cockles had to be left on the wharf by every vessel carrying these delicacies; boats fishing for salmon had to pay him an annual toll of 6s 8d; herring boats plying between Yarmouth and London paid twelve pence each trip; and there was a 'custom of two pence from every person going and returning by the River Thames on pilgrimage to the shrine of St James' . . . which was why we were there.

It is true we were about to sail from Plymouth rather than from

London, but having come across a couple of references to this charge on pilgrims – which no one seemed to have paid for some centuries – we had written to ask if we might be allowed to resurrect the custom.

The Resident Governor and Keeper of the Jewel House, Major-General Patrick MacLellan, invited us to tea in Queen's House (where he lived next to the Bloody Tower) and accepted my proffered 5p piece. When I told him that our four-year-old son Merlin was to accompany us he suggested, with a trace of the entrepreneurial spirit of his precursors, that he would accept 1p for the child as a fair due. But I explained that since he would be travelling in a car he could not be considered a proper pilgrim, and so I received my change.

Sir Walter Ralegh, the great English soldier, author and explorer, was locked up in the Tower by Queen Elizabeth and later by King James I. Cruelly and unjustly condemned to death for treason, Ralegh wrote a poem the night before his execution was planned. He called it 'The Passionate Man's Pilgrimage':

> Give me my scallop-shell of quiet,
> My staff of Faith to walk upon,
> My scrip of joy, immortal diet,
> My bottle of salvation,
> My gown of glory, hope's true gage,
> And thus I'll take my pilgrimage.*

Although Ralegh never went on the pilgrimage himself, this first verse is probably the most evocative and best known reference to it in English literature. The poetry deteriorates over the following six verses, but the symbolism continues, as does the wit and courage of the man. Reprieved at the last moment, he was confined for thirteen years before being released to lead another expedition to South America in search of gold. On his return, unsuccessful, he was finally beheaded in 1618 on the old charge, never having received a pardon. It was in the Bloody Tower that he wrote his *History of the World*, and it was there that the King's son, Prince Henry – who was to die before he could succeed to the throne – fell under his spell. 'Who but my father,' he wrote 'would shut up such a bird.'

The Governor showed us the dungeon in the White Tower where it is believed that my ancestor, Anne Askew, was racked in 1546 in an unsuccessful attempt to make her recant her Protestant heresy before being burned at the stake. Her story had fascinated me from earliest childhood. As I stood in the cold stone vault and listened to the silence, I asked the Governor if the Tower was haunted. 'This

* See Appendix 1 for complete poem.

place is full of memories and echoes of the past. How could it be otherwise?' he replied.

Anne's heresy was that she refused to accept the concept of transubstantiation, that the bread and wine of the sacrament are the very flesh and blood of Christ rather than – as she and subsequent Protestants would have it – symbols of the same. Nothing would make her say that what she believed to be true was not so. There is a vivid account of her racking and in the dungeon I tried to imagine how agonizing it must have been and how great her courage.

The Lieutenant at that time was Sir Anthonie Knevet. He seems to have been a decent, fair man who, when ordered by King Henry VIII to rack his prisoner so as to extract from her the names of any others who might think as she did, commanded his gaoler to do so. When he thought she had had enough, he was about to release her when the notorious persecuting Chancellor, Wriothesley, and Dr Rich, the Solicitor-General, arrived and insisted she be strained again. This Sir Anthonie refused to do, saying she was too weak to endure any more, at which the Chancellor and Dr Rich 'throwing off their gownes would needs play the tormentors themselves'. They worked the screws for a long time 'till her bones and joints almost were pluck't asunder' but she 'lai still and did not crie'.

The Dictionary of National Biography describes this incident as a glaring violation of the law, while the historian Froude says that it was 'perhaps the darkest page in the history of any English statesman'.

At last when it was over, they rode off on horses towards the Court; but the Lieutenant went by boat and reached the King first, begging his pardon and explaining what had happened. The King was not pleased to hear of 'so extreme handling of the woman and so granted to the Lieutenant his pardon, willing him to return and see to his charge'. However she was still burned at the stake at Smithfield with three others, a priest, a tailor and a gentleman.

Later under Queen Mary nearly 300 Protestants were to be burned at the stake, but in the time of Henry VIII it was fairly rare for anyone to be martyred in this way, let alone a woman. The story of her extraordinary courage and fortitude was widely told at the time and undoubtedly helped the Protestant cause. The ballad which she wrote and sang in Newgate was printed in Germany and smuggled back into England. The first verse is powerful stuff.

> Lyke as the armed knyght
> Appoynted to the fielde,
> With this world wyll I fyght
> And fayth shall be my shielde.*

* See Appendix 2 for complete poem.

My mother, who taught me herself in Ireland during the war until I was eight, used whatever books she had to hand. One of our favourites was Farjeon's *Heroes and Heroines*, delightful doggerel verses summing up the lives of legendary characters in history. I have an old notebook in which, at my request, she added a poem about our ancestor in the same style.

> In 1540 Anne Askew
> Had ideas which, then, were new
> (When Protestants whom she liked best,
> Had to have courage to protest).
>
> Anne, who said what she felt true,
> Never feared to argue.
> Which, in 1545,
> Was risky if you wished to thrive.
>
> So in 1546,
> With gun-powder and dry sticks,
> Prelates of the Church of Rome
> Helped her to an eternal home.
>
> Anne, whose faith defied the fire,
> Lived in fenny Lincolnshire;
> Let us, who can boast her blood,
> Have faith – and courage to be good.*

I had always wondered what courage and belief led someone who was clearly sane and full of the enjoyment of life to endure martyrdom for an article of faith. Would Christians go to the stake today over matters of dogma, and if not are there other passions which are held sufficiently strongly by their adherents that they would die for them?

To try to understand these questions was one of the reasons for my wanting to go on the pilgrimage. I suspected that the passion of the zealot, at least in the west, was more likely to be directed towards saving whales, elephants and rain forests from extinction than towards doctrinal principles. Being a fanatical enthusiast on some of these issues myself, I wished to speculate whether these feelings were as strong as those of my ancestor.

There were other less philosophical reasons too. The Way of St James leads through northern Spain across some of the most wild and beautiful country left in Europe, and yet, being an ancient track trodden by literally millions of feet over the last thousand years at least, it would not be difficult to follow. Moreover, along the Way some of Christendom's finest medieval architecture had been raised

* Ruth Tenison, 1943, written (by order) to amuse Robin aged six.

by the faithful. Built to serve the vast numbers of pilgrims who used to make the arduous journey across Europe by a variety of routes, the churches and monasteries of the final 500 miles were largely still there, while lesser hermitages and shrines – many ruined and forgotten – would greet us at almost every corner.

We wanted to go on another long ride together, and we wanted to take our youngest child with us. As soon as we decided to do so by going on the pilgrimage to Santiago de Compostela, a whole series of serendipitous coincidences made this inevitable. To list them all would be tedious and their relevance might seem tendentious, but I have never before made a journey which fell so naturally into place and which was planned and executed with such ease. My chief worry throughout was that the book which I had undertaken to write would be beyond me. It was not merely the physical and logistical problems which bothered me. There are already several excellent books about the pilgrimage to Santiago, notably that by Edwin Mullins, written in 1974, whose erudition and insight into the history and architecture of the route inspired me more than anything else to want to make the journey. There are also reference books and guides in Spanish, French and English which now carry most of the information needed to make the pilgrimage and see what should be seen. The fact that no one had written about riding to Santiago on a horse was not enough to justify a book. For me the motive had to be something much more personal, and I wondered what would happen. Our bishop in Cornwall, with whom I discussed my own growing heretical ideas, gave me the best advice. 'I shouldn't worry,' he said, 'just go and make the pilgrimage. You will find that by the time you reach Santiago you will know what it is you want to say.'

We sailed on the new ferry from Plymouth to Santander. This journey – across the Bay of Biscay from Cornwall, one of the recognized and frequently used routes to Santiago – used to be known as 'taking the cockleshell'. Anything less like a cockleshell than the *Bretagne* would be hard to imagine; she is a pearl among ferry-boats, all elegance and space, Art Deco and *haute cuisine*. The state-rooms deserved honeymoon couples, the staff were helpful, friendly and mostly French. The sea was like a duck-pond.

How very different it was in the 15th century when what has been called the first sea shanty was written. 'The Pilgrims Sea Voyage and Sea Sickness' describes one of the crowded dreadful journeys across the Bay of Biscay, when passengers suffered terribly as they lay in the holds of wine ships returning to Bordeaux or in one of the many vessels which sailed direct to Corunna, taking pilgrims virtually the whole way in five days or so. In those days the crew members were unfriendly and teased the pilgrims that they would be sick:

> Bestowe the boote, Bote-swayne, anon,
> That our pylgryms may play theron;
> For som ar lyke to cowgh and grone
> Or hit be full mydnyght.

Soon enough the prophecy was fulfilled, especially when the sailors were brought food. All the pilgrims wanted was hot Malmsey.

> Thys mene whyle the pylgryms ly,
> And haue theyr bowlys fast theym by,
> And cry aftyr hote maluesy;
> Thow helpe for to restore.

And sleep gave no release . . .

> For when that we shall go to bedde,
> The pumpe was nygh oure beddes hede,
> A man were as good to be dede
> As smell therof the stynk!*

Our crossing took only twenty-four hours to Santander, from which it was only a few hours' drive through wildly contrasting Spanish countrysides of seascape, mountain, desert and rich farmland to Roncesvalles, where we were to start our pilgrimage.

The route followed by pilgrims to the north-west tip of Spain was once the busiest trunk road in Christendom, to which hundreds of thousands of them came each year from all over Europe. Some estimates put the figure as high as two million a year, though the half-million calculated for one year in the 12th century is probably nearer the mark. Nonetheless, these figures can be compared with the annual influx of tourists to the *costas* of Spain today and, when set against the vast increase in European population since the Middle Ages, it is true to say that proportionately medieval pilgrims greatly exceeded modern tourists. Pilgrimage was very big business.

The pilgrimage made Santiago de Compostela the third holiest city in Christendom, after Jerusalem and Rome, and the easiest to visit. Northern Italy had become infested with robbers and bandits, making travel to Rome highly dangerous, although every bishop was supposed to go there after his consecration; while to reach the Holy Land, even as a member of one of the Crusades, must have been extremely hazardous and time-consuming.

The urge to travel and to visit holy places is not confined to Christians. There had been *peregrines,* wanderers, pilgrims on the roads of Europe at least since the Emperor Constantine adopted Christianity in the 4th century and probably long before that, but it was not until the 10th century that the practice really caught on

* The Pilgrims Sea Voyage (Verons MS., ab 1370, Bodleian Library) ed F.J. Furnival.

and became something of an obsession with them. Mecca was already the spiritual centre of Islam, and one of the reasons for Santiago becoming so important was the need to find a Christian shrine of equal importance. Interestingly, both places had been considered holy and were the object of veneration and pilgrimage long before Christianity or Islam came on the scene. The Black Stone and the Ka'ba (cube) at Mecca had been worshipped as idols for centuries by Arab tribes, who walked around the sacred building seven times just as modern Muslim pilgrims do today.

Like the other western extremities of Europe, Finisterre – the region around Compostela – is rich in dolmens and traces of ancient gods, worshipped perhaps because of their closeness to the setting sun. It seems probable that prehistoric religions included westward migrations among their rituals and that the legends associated with the tradition became, as was so often the case, entwined in Christian mythology. The Milky Way stretching from east to west across the heavens was seen as a celestial reflection of the Way of St James. Folklore confused Jesus and his brother – in reality the other St James, the Less – with Castor and Pollux, the Heavenly Twins whose constellation Gemini lies in the Milky Way. Castor (famed incidentally for his horsemanship) and his brother were worshipped by the Greeks and later in Rome where their cult dates from the 5th century B.C. An early Roman road, traces of which still exist, led to Compostela. The name itself was believed, probably erroneously, to derive from *campus stellae*, the field of the star, giving rise to all kinds of romantic associations with Wise Men and the following of stars. In fact modern scholars say that the name probably comes from Compostum, meaning a cemetery. And this does seem more likely, since the whole myth of St James in Spain arose from the highly questionable discovery at the beginning of the 9th century of a body identified as that of the saint.

None of this mattered to the pilgrims who flooded westward from the millennium onwards, revelling in the visual and mental experiences of the journey while expiating their sins, gaining indulgences and surely, in most cases, having the greatest experience of their lives.

Those who came by ship have been described as the first sea passengers ever, which cannot be true if one thinks of the Chinese, Egyptians, Greeks and Romans. Perhaps 'the first mass market group travellers' would be a fairer description. Those who walked or rode to Santiago were described by Dante as the only true 'pilgrims', though he also said that anyone travelling away from home may be called a pilgrim. However those who journeyed to Palestine were (he wrote) properly called Palmers because they brought back palm-branches; while those who went to Rome were called Romers. He was writing a century before Chaucer, whose pilgrims were of course heading for the shrine of St Thomas à Becket at Canterbury. The word canter, originally a Canterbury gallop, comes from the steady gait of mounted pilgrims on their way to that cathedral.

The token carried to Santiago by pilgrims was and still is the scallop-shell – to show where they were going and to prove where they had been. Those who had been on several pilgrimages would sometimes cover their hats and clothes with the relevant badges; there is a description of such a one in *Piers Plowman:*

> A hundred of vials was set on his hat,
> Signs from Sinai, gallician shells;
> With crosses on his cloak, and the keys of Rome,
> And the Vernicle before, for that men should discern
> And see by his signs what shrines he had sought.

They also carried the staff and scrip to which Ralegh refers in his poem. All these accoutrements combined utility with symbolism. The staff had a pointed metal tip like an alpenstock, which was useful in rough country and as a weapon when fending off wild animals and savage dogs. Allegorically these came to represent the snares of the devil. A pilgrim's prayer goes: 'Be to them, O Lord, a defence in danger, a port in shipwreck, a diversion in the journey, a shade in the intense heat, a light in darkness, a staff in carnal temptation . . .' It also symbolized the Trinity, being the pilgrim's third leg.

The scrip was usually a wallet of soft leather, today's rucksack, but then carried open as both a practical and a symbolic way of giving or receiving alms, since charity was always integral to pilgrimage whether as donor or beneficiary.

The scallop itself was the pilgrim's dish or spoon, with which he could help himself to communal stews in hospices along the Way, or drink from streams. The shell symbolized spiritual protection; it was considered to have magical powers, to cure sickness and to ward off the evil eye.

The pilgrimage was popularized and encouraged by a remarkable book, the famous *Codex Calixtinus* which was probably edited and written in part by a monk called Aymery Picaud from Parthenay-le-Vieux, near Poitiers, in about 1139. The French Pope Calixtus II, to whom this book was falsely attributed, was crowned at the great Benedictine monastery at Cluny, which was then larger than St Peter's in Rome. With its 300 dependancies, the Cluniac order was largely responsible for developing the Christian enthusiasm of the period for going on Crusades and for uniting to drive the Moors from Spain. The Cluniacs pioneered the route to Santiago, building churches along the Way and bearing the scallop-shell on their coat of arms. Pope Calixtus gave the indulgences and privileges to the first Archbishop of Compostela, which made the cathedral rich and powerful, thus confirming its right to be compared with Rome and Jerusalem.

The *Codex* was written in five books, the first three of which in turn dealt with sermons and hymns, miracles and legends connected with St James. The fourth is devoted to an epic song about Charlemagne's campaigns in Spain. The fifth has been called the first tourist guide ever written and it describes the countryside and people, the rivers and routes, the shrines and relics to be found on the Way. It is full of French chauvinism, reeking of dislike and distrust for the Basques and Spaniards to be met – and, if possible, avoided – by pilgrims en route. But it is also full of vivid word pictures describing the atmosphere and experiences enjoyed by a 12th-century pilgrim. The 500 miles which we were about to ride were divided into thirteen stages. Even if, as was probably the case, they were designed to inspire mounted pilgrims, the length of each stage makes it hard to believe that anyone was seriously expected to cover one per day. We were to take exactly twice as long, and we were able to travel light.

Our horses came from Señor Pablo Hermoso de Mendoza of Estella. We had shaken hands the previous May on a deal whereby he would deliver two good animals to us at Roncesvalles and collect them from Santiago a month later. The cost was less than we would probably lose if we attempted to buy and then sell at the end – which would in any case have been very difficult with all the hysteria about African Horse Sickness – and we were relieved of the worry.

We pitched our tents in a grassy meadow beside the stream below the great monastery at Roncesvalles and waited anxiously for them to arrive. Joan and Merlin were going to use one tent, while the other was ours. Joan had looked after Merlin almost from his birth and, having a grandson of the same age who was his best friend, was more like a much-loved grandmother than a nanny. When he was only a year old we had left him with her for four months while we rode along the Great Wall of China; and again eighteen months later for two months, while we rode through New Zealand. We had missed him dreadfully on both occasions, but thanks to Joan's affection and good sense he survived the separations without apparently missing us much. A year previously she had been accepted as one of only four mature students by Falmouth College of Art. Now her foundation course was finished and she had earned her diploma, which included photography. Therefore apart from driving our support vehicle and finding somewhere for us and the horses to stay each night, she was to take all the black and white photographs.

We were also joined for the first few days by Jane Rabagliati, the

First Secretary at the British Embassy in Madrid responsible for agriculture. She had been extraordinarily helpful over our horse arrangements, being a knowledgeable horsewoman herself and an *aficionado* of the Andalusian or Spanish horse. We knew our mounts would not be members of that noble breed, but Jane had discussed our needs at length in her fluent Spanish with Pablo, and we were confident that he would not let us down. She had also taken the trouble to get her Minister to write to the head of the Guardia Civil, recommending us to them and enclosing our proposed itinerary. This had resulted, she told us, in an official letter being sent to every Guardia Civil post along our route instructing them to help us. Even though we had no intention of calling on this generosity, it was hugely reassuring to know it was there should anything go wrong.

The massive grey monastery building, usually described as grim and ugly, was bathed in warm August sunshine and silhouetted against the evening light. Surrounded by great beeches, it towered over us, romantic as a fairy tale and not at all the soulless place we had been led to expect. Padre Javier Navarro, the sub-prior in charge of pilgrims, had issued us with our 'passports' when we called on him. Only pilgrims who walk or ride bicycles or horses are entitled to these, and they must be stamped regularly at churches or town halls along the route in order to qualify the bearer for a 'Compostela' or certificate that the pilgrimage has been duly completed. These have been issued since the 14th century and at one time there was quite a trade in them at just this spot, where pilgrims who had survived the rigours of the Pyrenees were now faced with a gruelling 500 miles of wild country. The padre, who was talkative, friendly and eager to help the first pilgrims this year to write '*caballo*' against 'method of travel', had directed us down to the meadow by the stream. 'Go a little way upstream,' he urged. 'The water there is pure enough to drink, as you will be above the *cloacas*.' The Spanish word for sewer is the same in English and indeed Latin, but I had not heard it used in this context since I had last stayed at a monastery – the 11th-century Simonas Petras – thirty-five years before on Mount Athos. It was built high on a pinnacle of cliff over the Aegean, with rickety wooden balconies around the sides. The *cloaca* to which a kindly monk directed me, after we had struggled to communicate in a variety of ancient and modern languages, was a round hole in one of the highest and least stable galleries. As I crouched clinging to a worn hand-rail, shiny from the daily clasp of monastic hands, I could see below me seagulls and, hundreds of feet below them, waves crashing on to the rocks.

Charlemagne, the great King of the Franks and later Holy Roman Emperor, invaded Spain in 778. He did so for strictly territorial reasons, and rather unsuccessfully besides, but he started the very slow process by which the Moors were eventually to be expelled 700 years later. There was in fact an Islamic presence in Spain for more years (781) than have elapsed since the last Moor was expelled from Granada in 1492. For about 500 of those years they ruled most of the country.

The more significant outcome of a Christian king's incursion into Spain, however, was that it made a potential pilgrimage route through the hostile north of the country more possible than before. Subsequent legends were to relate how St James came to Charlemagne in a dream and bade him search for his tomb, which had not then been discovered. The greatest and perhaps most imaginative of all the legends concerned the retreat from Spain, when the rearguard of his army was attacked as it was crossing the Pyrenees at Roncesvalles. This was and still is in the heart of Basque country; they have always been a fierce and proud people who resented anyone invading their country, especially someone who had just knocked down the walls of their capital Pamplona, which lay just to the west. They massacred Charlemagne's great warriors – notably Roland, his nephew, immortalized through the *Song of Roland*, the first French epic poem, parts of which were sung by the Norman minstrel Taillefer to encourage the Conqueror's troops at the Battle of Hastings nearly 300 years later. Over subsequent centuries, pilgrims were entertained by singers who embellished the story outrageously as they played their hurdy-gurdys.*

Since so much of the motive for the pilgrimage was bound up in the desire to rid Spain of the Moors, a kind of peaceful Crusade, it was hardly surprising that Roland's attackers became 100,000 perfidious Saracens, who ambushed him and whom he bravely fought and killed with his trusty and unbreakable sword Durendal; but by then he had only fifty men left and when suddenly another 50,000 Moors appeared he knew he was doomed. Desperately he blew a mighty blast on his enchanted ivory horn, Olifant. The sound was so loud that birds fell dead and the enemy were terror-struck. Beyond the wooded pass, Charlemagne heard the horn and wanted to rush to his aid, but the wicked Ganelon – who had arranged the whole thing – persuaded him that Roland was only hunting deer. At the third blast the horn cracked in two. Mortally wounded, Roland tried to break Durendal on a boulder so that it should not fall into enemy hands, but he only succeeded in splitting the rock in half, thus providing a wonderful site for pilgrims to gasp at as they struggled over the Brèche de Roland† centuries later. Desperately he

* See Appendix 3.
† This is another pass some 150 kms to the east of Roncesvalles, where a huge cleft does indeed rend the rocky ridge.

threw Durendal into a poisoned stream before he died, and it has lain there ever since. Perhaps it was the very same stream beside which we were camped. The whole story is highly reminiscent of Arthur and his magic sword Excalibur which, as everyone knows, was cast by Sir Bedivere into Dozmary Pool on Bodmin Moor about five miles as the raven flies from our farm. People are less likely to know, however, that Runcible Spoons, which have three prongs – one with a sharp cutting edge useful for dealing with 'mince and slices of quince' – are said, according to *Brewer*, 'to be so called in humorous reference to the slaughter (with sharp swords) at Ronces-valles'.

Our horses arrived just as we finished erecting the tents and were led towards us by Jane and Pablo's son Juan-Andres, with Merlin racing alongside in high excitement. We waited agog as they skirted the monastery walls and drew near. To our relief, both were greys with long manes and tails. There had been talk that Louella's horse might have a docked tail, and for once she had put her foot down saying that if such was the case she would go home. They were not pure Andalusians by a very long way, and they were thinner than we could have wished, but they seemed calm and good-natured and Juan-Andres assured us that they would get to Santiago. Jane looked doubtful. Mine was called Duque – after the Duke of Wellington, I chose to believe, who drove Napoleon out of Spain in the Peninsular War. There could hardly be a more appropriate name for an English pilgrim's horse. Louella's, also a gelding, was called Guadalquivir after the main river of southern Spain. The name derives from the Moorish for 'the great river' Wadi al Kebir. He was much more sensible than Duque and preferred to lead, so Juan-Andres told us.

We fastened them to corkscrew pickets which I had brought from England. These were designed to anchor unruly dogs out shooting, but – being trained not to try to escape – the horses seldom pulled them, nor did they often allow the twenty feet or so of rope to tangle around their legs. On the rare occasions when this did happen they sensibly stood still until help arrived, instead of panicking as most other horses, including our Camargues, would have done.

The bell from the Royal Collegiate Church tolled and we hurried across the hillside for the pilgrim mass at 8 o'clock. Before entering the jumble of buildings we looked back to see our two white steeds grazing contentedly beside our two tents, set in an idyllic grassy meadow below the great wooded Pyrenees. It was a good moment.

Nine priests in white robes embroidered with green pilgrim crosses officiated in turn, sitting in a semi-circle in front of the high altar whose gilded canopy arched above the object venerated by all pilgrims who have passed that way during the 750 years since the church was founded. The charming 13th-century Virgin of Ronces-

valles sits holding her child, both silver-plated to protect the carved
wood beneath, but cheerful and alert as though encouraging travellers through the rigours ahead. And that was the purpose of the
service. There was a congregation of about fifty, contrasting sharply
between the mostly elderly locals in sober, respectable clothes and
the young pilgrims in anoraks, shorts and trainers. The singing was
excellent, led by the priests who moved about with consummate
dignity to deliver prayers and homilies appropriate to those setting
out on a long journey, to give us all communion and to bless us.
Looking up at the candlelight glinting on the golden columns and
illuminating the red hangings behind, while the robed figures
changed places, their arms folded in front of them, a sense of timelessness and history swept over me. I began to feel a strength and
conviction that what we were doing was right, whatever our motives.
I had worried before that perhaps it was wrong to go on a pilgrimage
without proper spiritual preparation, regular church attendance and
a suitably penitential frame of mind. Now I felt an endorsement that
the journey itself was enough to begin with. Our bishop had told
me not to worry and now I just wanted to start. If it led me into
heretical thoughts, then that need not be a negative act; in fact it
would be the very opposite. Otherwise, why bother with speculation
at all? Pilgrimage today is a highly ecumenical affair. Even Padre
Navarro, the canon hospitaler – now so solemn and dignified in his
vestments – had asked us brightly when issuing our 'passports' to
tick a list of motives for our pilgrimage; a list which included as I
recall tourism, sport and culture as well as religion. In 1987 the
Council of Europe had chosen the pilgrim route to Santiago 'as a
symbol of the European identity, within which so many cultures and
nations are included'.

The spiritual feelings engendered by ritual, sonorous singing,
organ music and fellowship such as we were experiencing is available
to all at all times, whatever their beliefs. I love church ritual, but I
do not have to believe everything I am told. It is the essence of
Protestantism not to do so. Through the ages it has been the lot of
thinking men and women to question dogma and thus attempt both
to keep the Church in line and change it to adapt to new circum-
stances. This was a dangerous duty, especially when the Inquisition
flourished as it did in Spain for nearly 600 years. I felt a moment
of angst as the priests' shadows leapt across the nave and their
bowed heads seemed to be both cowled and reading my thoughts.

Then those of us who were pilgrims were being summoned to
come forward and stand before the altar to receive our blessings.
These were delivered in Spanish and French and are a most important rite, dating from at least the 10th century. Normally they would
have taken place in the pilgrim's own parish church, or perhaps in

front of his bishop; he would have prostrated himself before the altar and at the end of the ceremony received a staff and scrip which had been blessed. If he was taking the pilgrimage to expiate some grave crime such as murder he might be branded with a cross or have a tau, a T, cut into his forehead and be wrapped in a chain forged from the murder weapon before setting out. The object of all was to return joyfully, with sins forgiven.

We stood in a row and listened as we were exhorted to make our journeys in a due spirit of reverence, God's blessing and protection were sought on our behalf and we were sent on our way. We never saw any of the other thirty or so pilgrims again. They must all have been bicyclists or even, heaven forbid, travellers by vehicle who should not have been there at all.

That night Merlin slept with us while Jane shared Joan's tent. The horses grazed a steep grassy bank to which we moved them, tree frogs chirped loudly, at least two species of owl called to each other in the woods and the stream splashed noisily past. In the middle of the night Merlin woke up and asked us to switch it off!

NAVARRA

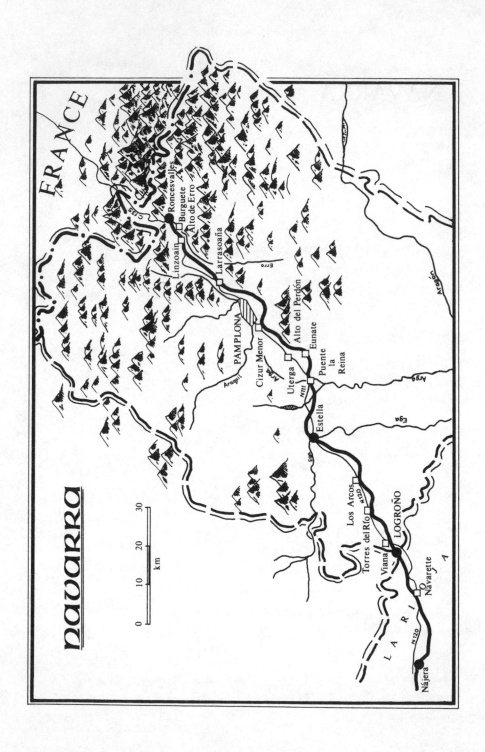

Who would true valour see
Let him come hither;
One here will constant be,
Come wind, come weather;
There's no discouragement
Shall make him once relent
His first avow'd intent
    To be a pilgrim.

Whoso beset him round
With dismal stories,
Do but themselves confound;
His strength the more is.
No lion can him fright;
He'll with a giant fight,
But he will have the right
    To be a pilgrim.

No goblin nor foul fiend
Can daunt his spirit;
He knows he at the end
Shall life inherit.
Then, fancies, fly away;
He'll not fear what men say;
He'll labour night and day
    To be a pilgrim.

DAY 1 Wednesday 9th August   RONCESVALLES TO LARRASOAÑA

Waking early and slipping out of our tent before it was light, I sat on the bank beside the stream and watched the day dawn. The first anxious look uphill found the horses grazing peacefully on their pickets. Mist lay in our valley, dwarfing our little tents, and there was a chill in the air as I shaved and washed. Rain must have fallen high in the Pyrenees during the night as our stream had risen and dropped again, leaving a trail of sticks and leaves within inches of the tent. One of the first lessons I learnt when travelling in the Sahara was never to camp in a wadi in case of flash floods. Now I felt foolish, but worse was to come.

Thinking I would water the horses before anyone else woke up, I released Duque from his picket and led him towards the stream. Suddenly I was up to my waist in cold mud and floundering desperately as I tried to escape. Luckily Duque had neither followed me nor panicked when I disappeared and I still held the rope attached to his head collar. He was rolling his eyes and backing away, however, which helped to pull me out. I pride myself on being able to spot bogs – an upbringing in Ireland saw to that – but the one into which I had walked really was invisible, caused by a trickle down the hillside being dammed by the track. It also stank and I suspected the *cloacas* of having access to it. The clean jeans which I had put on for our first day's riding were black and slimy, and to complete my chagrin Louella chose that moment to poke her head out of the tent-flap and suggest I wait until she helped me with the horses. I waited shivering while she dressed and fetched Guadalquivir, but when we reached the water neither horse would drink, even though we led them well upstream. I stripped off and washed myself and my clothes in a deeper pool. By the time I had finished that, the first-day nerves from which I had been suffering since waking were effectively exorcized and I felt ready for anything. As the time approaches, it is always hard to believe that all the planning and hopes leading up to the moment of departure will not be dashed by unforeseen disaster. Experiencing a minor one somehow reassured me that all would be well from then on.

While the others made coffee on Joan's small gas primus and started to break camp, I went up to the monastery. The paddock we were camped in was locked and we needed the key before we could leave. It was still early and there was no one about. We were to find that the Spanish are late risers even in the country, but I was eager to set off and so searched the buildings. Then I heard singing from the church and went in. This time there was no congregation and instead of candlelight the rising sun was flooding through the stained glass and the wine-red hangings below. The nine canons, their green and white habits now suffused in a red glow, sat in a semi-circle behind the altar and they sang together in harmony without benefit of organ, a beautiful Gregorian chant. It was a scene straight out of the Middle Ages and the deep spirituality of the moment was tangible. The theatre was for themselves and for God. I should not have been there.

Mystical communion through song and ritual tends to be glossed over in the Anglican Church. It is even seen as faintly embarrassing and suspect – smells and bells – but it is at the heart of much faith. Of course there are plenty of other ways in which people achieve religious ecstasy, through asceticism, inspired preaching and many more, but in the church at Roncesvalles I felt I was seeing one of the purest forms.

I sat for a while invisible at the back of the church and watched the priests at their devotions. It is easy to lose oneself at such moments, to be carried along unthinking on the tide of ritual. This is the level of experience which moves me through the major ecclesiastical events of my life, the responsible solemnity of baptism, the emotional happiness at weddings, grief at funerals. We all feel these things, however stiff our upper lips pretend to be, and religious ritual helps us to deal with them.

At another level there are the moments of crisis when belief suddenly becomes significant as I pray to my personal God, even striking bargains and promising to do something or give something up if the imminent disaster is miraculously averted. These bargains are as much with myself as an external deity, yet still there is something I believe in, something greater than my own flesh and blood. Science and pragmatism are not enough; there must be more. The trouble is that the rituals and sets of rules no longer satisfy my concerns about life. The Christian virtues of goodness and gentleness are fine as a moral philosophy, but I object to the insistence that I must believe a whole lot of things which to me are patently nonsense. If I belonged to one of the more extreme Christian sects – as an evangelical fundamentalist, say – I would doubtless have been shocked by the scene before me, seeing it as the Devil at work. Likewise the Church of Rome regards Protestantism in all its forms as heretical. This whole long battle seems out of date and pointless to me; the issues are irrelevant today and certainly not worth going to the stake for. Intellectually and practically, I am no longer interested in the debate. Instead there are burning issues affecting the future of mankind and of all life on earth which are of great immediacy and demand that petty dogmatic rivalries be set aside. The solutions with which I feel easiest are Gaian. James Lovelock, who lives on Bodmin Moor not far from us, first proposed this new theory of life only ten years ago. He says that for him Gaia is 'a religious as well as a scientific concept'. He rejects undiluted faith, being too deeply committed to science. Each of us must find his or her own relationship with Gaia and it suits me to believe that, in addition to working as a holistic, self-regenerating unity, there is a mind behind it all which understands and with which each living thing has a special relationship. Whether this mind is internal and corporal in some way we cannot begin to understand, or extraterrestial, which has always been the general view of heaven long before science fiction, does not really matter; it is the belief in it that matters. Religion has been well defined as a belief in super-human power, from which stems a desire to do the right thing, to serve it properly. For Jews, Christians and Muslims the service of an unearthly mind takes varying but broadly similar forms, the observation of laid-down rules. Today these rules seem irrelevant to many, but instead of being rejected and replaced by crass self-interest and materialism, a new green philosophy is emerging. According to 'green' rules it is as important as ever to lead a 'good' life; only the criteria of what are good things to do have changed. Instead of being preoccupied with the salvation of one's own soul, or obsessed with the need to save others, the green pilgrim is concerned with the welfare and survival of all forms of life, including his own. Indeed, he sees the two as inexorably intertwined.

There was a gratifying sense of occasion about our departure from Roncesvalles. We rode through a low archway into a central court-yard where young people camped in tents were just getting dressed. In our shirts, on which Louella had stencilled scallop-shells, there could be no doubt about where we were going. On our black Camargue hats we had silver replicas of a medieval scallop badge found in the Thames. The horses had splendid *mosqueros* on their foreheads, each containing a real scallop-shell; Jane had had these made up specially for us in Madrid. Without the shell they are part of the correct rig of a properly turned-out working Andalusian horse, the plaited tassels swinging from side to side with the horse's action to keep away the flies. The scallop-shell is particularly appropriate on a horse, since one legend has it that when St James's body was being brought ashore in a stone boat at Padrón, a horse bolted into the sea with its rider, emerging from the waves miraculously unscathed and draped in scallop shells.

Through a dark passage where we had to duck our heads, past the church door and out on to the grassy lawn where tourists were gathering to see the monastery. The priest of the day blessed us and pointed us on our way to Santiago, the tourists clapped and clicked furiously with their cameras and Merlin, who had also been issued with a pilgrim 'passport', ran beside us until stopped by the main road. We crossed it – following the first of the yellow arrows mark-ing the Old Way, which we were to become Pavlovian in our instinc-tive urge to follow – and plunged into a wood. A leafy glade, our first gentle Canterbury gallop and a huge lifting of our spirits as we realized that they were good brave horses and everything was going to be all right. Another major relief came when we reached the first wire fences between woods and meadows and found that beside each stile for the many walkers who had gone before us was a gate of some sort for rare riders like us. Bicyclists were confined to roads, walkers could follow the rough old track but had to slog along under their packs with eyes cast down to watch where they put their feet; but we would have the best of all worlds, being free to enjoy the scenery. Nothing along the way ahead was to exceed in pastoral pleasantness the Basque countryside through which we rode that first day. Solid white buildings with wide gabled pantile roofs and red shutters and doors, set in lush green fields in which grazed fat brown cows – it was like an illustration in a child's picture book.

Burguete, the first village we came to, was where (in *The Sun Also Rises*) Ernest Hemingway describes spending a week fishing. Each day Barnes, the narrator, and his friend Bill would walk over the ridge to the east, fish in the Río Irati and return in the evening laden with trout. I doubt if the river is as well stocked today as it was just after the First World War.

The Basques' legendary industriousness and pride in their territory showed itself with each new prospect. The villages through which we rode were clean and looked scrubbed; there were bright geraniums in pots hanging from balconies, and many of the houses bore carved stone coats of arms. Just to be born a Basque used to be enough to secure nobility. In Linzoain we paused to water the horses at a stone trough beside the *fronton*, the extraordinarily high-walled court where the Basque national ball game of *pelota* – known in the western hemisphere as *jai alai* – is played. Reputedly the fastest game in the world, the ball – which is made of special wild Brazilian rubber wrapped in two layers of goatskin and propelled from a wicker basket glove – often exceeds 150 miles an hour through the air. The spectators bet heavily and almost every village we saw had a court of some sort, if only the wall of the church, on which the game's markings were painted. There were also frequent graffiti supporting ETA, which stands for Freedom for the Basques in their incomprehensible and unique language, for this was the heartland of their support. The Guardia Civil are the main targets of this small extremist group and we were assured that we had nothing to fear. The days when the Basques were notorious for plundering travellers and exploiting the pilgrims who passed through their lands are long gone.

We rode through meadows and thickets of hazel, up steep rocky lanes into the ancient woods of oak and beech which blanket the higher hills. At the Alto de Erro, the pass where the main road crosses the pilgrim Way, we stopped to rest the horses and let the sun dry their backs. This was something we would try to do each day to help combat saddle-sores, the great bugbear of the long-distance rider. I was alarmed to see that Duque already had a small sore place forming next to a scratch on his back which we had noticed when he arrived. I painted some scarlet mercurichrome on it: liquid which made the wound look much worse than it really was and stained everything with which it came in contact, but which dried and healed it remarkably fast.

After an hour we saddled up again and now had to lead the horses down a steep, wooded hillside where strange rock formations looked at times like the foundations of houses and where it was hard on all our feet. Louella was wearing a lovely old pair of leather cavalry boots which looked and felt excellent when riding but rubbed when walking. Since we were to do a lot of walking, both when crossing rough or steep terrain and to spare the horses, she was not able to wear them often but found trainers more comfortable.

After the beauty and freshness of the woods it was a shock to come out into baking sunshine and a view of a supremely ugly cement works. A hideous jumble of grey prefabricated buildings, pipes, tanks, overhead power-lines and slurry pits, all belching dust and smoke; the worst and arguably the least necessary of man's pollutants. There is little that cement can do which good stone-work cannot. The great medieval builders barely used mortar, and who would dare to say that any of the pre-cast carbuncles of the 20th century will outlast the great Romanesque and Gothic buildings we were to see daily along our route? Lasting and beautiful construction of this kind is far more labour intensive, of course, but are not over-population and unemployment among the world's greatest problems? As we picked our way through the litter and barren moonscape around the factory, the message was rammed home for us by the total absence of any visible human life among the noisy conveyors and hoppers impersonally moving sand about.

Once away from the din we were back in pretty farmland, where deep secret valleys were full of undergrowth and we had to bend low in our saddles to scrape through. Between were stubble fields where we could let our horses have their heads. The Río Arga flowed below us on our right and the hamlets we passed through had water-troughs, appealing old stone houses with vines growing up the walls and friendly people who waved to us from their balconies.

Then another horror spoiled the idyllic afternoon. There was a row of long modern buildings from which a low continuous hum emanated, and which we thought at first must be some sort of machinery. Then we heard the lone crowing of a cockerel rising above the background noise and realized that it was the frenetic babbling of thousands of caged chickens. To feed the ever-growing population of the Third and the ever-growing appetites of the First Worlds, it may be necessary to resort to such inhumane agricultural practices. But in the rolling Navarre foothills of the Pyrenees, where so much has been saved of the manifest contentment of village life, I was shocked. For the rest of the day that one brave rooster's call haunted me. Like Roland's desperate blast on Olifant, it seemed like a cry for help.

At Larrasoaña we crossed the Arga by an ivy-covered bridge and met Joan, Jane and Merlin, who had found a good camp-site close by. Under the bridge a large pool had been dammed, where the village children swam and played. We rode the horses in among them to their great delight, then unsaddled, stripped off and washed them and ourselves in the cool and, it must be said, rather smelly water.

The *alcalde*, or mayor, had said we could put our tents on the green next to the river, and there was plenty of grass under the trees for the horses. They had nosebags, too, in which their daily ration of five kilos each of a mixture of oats and barley was munched conveniently morning and evening.

I was sent to chat to the *alcalde* while supper was being prepared and to see if I could scrounge some salt, since ours had vanished. Señor Santiago Zubiri Elizalde was a most likeable and enthusiastic man, proud of what was being done to promote the pilgrimage route, known in Spain as the *Camino Francés* since most pilgrims had always come from France. His first comment was that the cement factory was much to be regretted and a diversion of the Way was planned. He presented us with a splendid illustrated map of the route through Navarre, with English text and pictures of the different types of pilgrim from motor cyclists to walkers and even showing a pair of horsemen. The Pope was due to pay a visit to Compostela at the end of the following week, when a vast number of pilgrims would gather to see him. Many had gone along part or all of the Way of St James ahead of us, and a big effort had been made to clear and mark it. Riding just after the main flood, we were to benefit from this.

We feasted heedlessly on chicken and noodles and a bottle of good local wine, sitting on the river bank while distant lightning lit the darkening sky. 'There are summer storms at this time of year,' said Jane, 'but it doesn't feel like rain tonight.' And we all agreed with her. But soon after everyone was tucked up in the tents there was a crash of thunder and raindrops started to patter on the canvas. Worried that the horses might panic, Louella and I crawled out to calm them. I noticed that Guadalquivir's picket was half out of the ground, which was stony and so a good deal of strength was needed to screw it in. I fetched a stick to give me some leverage and just as the storm broke, bringing a gale and torrential rain accompanied by almost continuous thunder and sheet lightning, the top of the picket snapped. Louella led her horse off to find somewhere to tie him, while I hurried towards mine to calm him. At that moment the big pine tree above our heads seemed to fall apart and huge branches crashed down all around us. Miraculously they hit neither us nor the horses, but the stump of the picket was completely buried by the branches and had it not broken someone would certainly have been hurt.

When the horses were settled again, we went back to the tent, soaked and suddenly very cold. Stripping off inside as the rain still poured down all round, we rubbed each other warm and dry with towels and put on dry clothes. We had a small candle lantern hanging from the ridge-pole to give light in the tent; Louella accidentally took hold of it and burned her hand quite badly, leaving a round black mark on her palm. The best treatment was to hold it under running water, which she could easily do by simply sticking it out through the flap into the heavy rain. But when she came to zip up the flap again, she caught her hair in it and it took us twenty minutes to get it free. Just on midnight the *alcalde* arrived under a black umbrella and asked us if we would like to move to the refuge in the schoolhouse. It was very kind of him, but by then it was all over.

DAY 2 Thursday 10th August   LARRASOAÑA TO CIZUR MENOR

*B*efore the storm we had spread a light tarpaulin over our saddles, tack and horse-feed, and the tin trunks on the Volvo roof-rack had kept out the rain; but still it took a long time to sort out the devastation of the night. The tents would need drying before being packed up, but the joy of having a ground crew was that we could leave them to do it and ride off. We clattered back over the old bridge and were at once in open country again.

Bruce Chatwin, describing the Heavenly Horses of China, writes:

All religions have propounded a belief in an immortal soul which flies off after death, while some have believed it possible to pre-empt the inconvenience of death by arranging to fly off while the body still breathes, but the soul needs a vehicle – a chariot, a saddle or wings (and we must not forget that for 3,000 years a man came nearest to flight on a galloping horse). Our hobby-horses and merry-go-rounds are the last vestiges of the 'vehicles' in European folklore which helped one 'get out of oneself'.

This passage alone was enough to justify riding on our pilgrimage rather than slogging along on foot; and that morning, glad to be alive, we gave our horses their heads on the first stubble field and let them race. Sailing in a stiff breeze, skiing off piste through fresh powder snow, canoeing through white water all bring their own élan and sense of speed, but for me none can touch the freedom I know at full gallop.

Out of the corner of my eye I glimpsed a peregrine falcon flashing past on scimitar wings. They were one of the most sought after birds for falconry in the Middle Ages and, unlike most other hawks, they were not taken as young from the nest but instead were caught when travelling or on their peregrinations. Their name used to be synonymous with pilgrims or indeed travellers of any kind.

Having been nearly wiped out in Britain by pesticides, as the final link in the food chain and therefore the most vulnerable, they are now coming back. A pair has arrived on my farm in Cornwall. The first time I saw one, I thought a low-flying jet was coming down the valley. Then about thirty wood-pigeons in tight formation streaked past my head followed by the peregrine, which shot straight up in the air when it saw me, abandoning its prey which it had herded together and terrorized so as to be able to pick out the plumpest.

The exhilaration was short-lived. Soon we came on steep slopes where the track was inches wide, slippery after the rain and over-grown. The saddles caught on low branches, and in wooded valleys the trees were barely far enough apart to squeeze past. Once, leading Duque through a ditch, he unexpectedly jumped, knocking me back-wards into a big bramble patch and landing on top of me. Flounder-ing about among his feet, I cursed in a most unpilgrimlike way. Although he managed not to trample on me, I emerged with my arms and back bloody and scratched, looking as though I had been suitably scourged for my profanity.

An hour or so later we came out on the main road, which we now had to follow for a time since we had decided to ride around rather than through the centre of Pamplona. The verge was narrow or non-existent and the traffic fast and noisy. In these conditions it is safer to face the oncoming vehicles, riding on the left as walkers in Spain are constantly urged by road signs to do. On a horse this can still be very dangerous, however. If a truck was bearing down on us at full speed and something in the hedge should cause one of the horses to shy out into the road at the last moment, then death seemed certain.

Louella and Guadalquivir led off at a good regular slow trot, almost an amble and just as comfortable. Duque and I followed nervously, and as each car neared he seemed to stick his bottom out into its path. This has been the story with all my horses on all our rides, and I have come to the reluctant conclusion that I can no longer justify blaming them, although I do so volubly when it hap-pens. Louella's calmness must transmit itself to her mounts, while my nervousness – or as I prefer to see it, my fertile imagination – leads mine to worry. My solution was to carry a leafy twig in my right hand, wave it at approaching lunatics and tap Duque's backside when necessary.

We survived the Pamplona bypass and then spent some time lost in a great undulating treeless plain, where endless cornfields separ-ated small hill towns. One of the nicer things about riding in Spain is that, unlike those in most other European countries, the towns often do not sprawl so that there is open country right outside the city walls. The same goes for villages, farmers keeping their machinery and animals in houses there rather than close to their fields. The disadvantage is that there is seldom anyone of whom to ask the way, nor are there farmhouses to which one may deviate for directions.

In time we found ourselves back in the west of Pamplona passing through the university campus, where we rode through leafy academic groves of trees, greeted with interest and vivacity by the students, who at once recognized us as pilgrims and asked if we were really going all the way to Santiago. We did think we looked pretty good on our matching white steeds, with chaps and scallop-shells, and we always made a point of smiling and calling 'Hola!' to everyone we passed. It was fun to watch the sudden dawn of interest and pleasure as people recognized us as mounted pilgrims. Shyness, slowness or sheer lack of interest, on the other hand, quite often caused country people to ignore us completely, when we would feel a stab of rather shameful irritation at the lack of response.

Cizur Menor, a small hill town just outside Pamplona, was now visible and that was where we had arranged our rendezvous. We crossed the Pamplona–Madrid railway line, the horses stepping warily on the sleepers while we trod down the signal wires for them. I have a nightmare of a hoof being stuck in the rails and being unable to free it before the express roars up. But not this time, and we urged the tired animals up the last climb.

Our car was parked outside the main house in the village, a rather grand place called Tremendo with a courtyard behind, a large garden and two farms. Maribel Roncal, who greeted us warmly and insisted the horses should enter her smart garden and be tied to trees on the lawn, runs a refuge for pilgrims in an annex. In perfect English she made us welcome and told us that the others were having lunch in the restaurant across the square. It was 4.30 and we were hungry so, after giving the horses a good rub down and fitting their nose-bags, we made our way there and feasted on succulent roast goat.

Pamplona is the capital of Navarre and best known outside Spain for its encierro or 'running of the bulls' during the San Fermin festival in the second week of July each year. Then, early each morning for a week, the bulls which will fight later in the day are driven through the narrow medieval streets to the Plaza de Toros. Hemingway immortalized the fiesta, dramatically evoking the dust, blood, fear and passion surrounding it. He is at his most succinct in describing the cathedral: 'It was dim and dark and the pillars went high up, and there were people praying, and it smelt of incense, and there were some wonderful big windows.' There is a black marble bust of him in the square beside the bullring; little children were climbing over it as we passed.

We wanted to have our pilgrim 'passports' stamped and so accosted a priest in the gloom, who led us to a door marked Privado.

Knocking on this produced an old man whom we followed back across the nave to the sacristy, a huge ormolu, gilt and plush salon where, he told us solemnly, the archbishop would change his vestments. Great chests lined the walls and from a drawer in one of these he fetched a big bunch of keys. Then he crossed the chamber again to another tall pair of doors which proved to be a wardrobe lined with shelves. The official seals and their ink-pad were now revealed. Never again was such a performance to be made of the stamping, which all kinds of different people from mayors to bar owners seemed able to perform, so that sometimes it was not even necessary for us to dismount.

A service was in progress as we made our way back through the cathedral and quite a crowd had gathered. While the priest and his acolytes officiated before the altar with incense and bells, the congregation chatted and moved around, so that I was struck once again by the paradoxical contrast between the relaxed atmosphere of the Catholic mass and the supposedly lower, less traditional and therefore, one would have expected, less formal services of Protestantism.

DAY 3 Friday 11th August   **CIZUR MENOR TO ESTELLA**

The hill villages rose above the early morning mist like islands and it was pleasantly cool for a while. We relished the freshness, knowing that the day to come would be long and by all the signs very hot. We were out of the mountains now, and between the successive ranges of hills which lay ahead there would be scorching open plains.

There is no road to the romantically named Guendulain and no one lives there any more; all that remains is just an abandoned fortified farmhouse, once the palace of the eponymous earls, and a church on a ridge. The track through the fields was silent and deserted. We had the day and, it seemed, the whole of Spain to ourselves.

'Do you realize,' Louella said, 'that we haven't seen a single other pilgrim since leaving Roncesvalles?' At that moment we spotted two young men in shorts and with large rucksacks sitting in the shade of a ruined wall. '*Hola*,' they said together. '*Que tal?*' '*Vous êtes Français?*' I asked, since they did not look Spanish. '*No, Inglés*,' they replied, and we soon discovered that they had both just come down from University College, Oxford. Nor were they pilgrims, being on their way from Bordeaux to Santander, walking some 500 kilometres 'for the exercise' in ten days. Julian was due at Sandhurst in a couple of weeks to join the regiment of which Louella's elder brother was Colonel. He had also apparently been at a party given by friends of ours in Cornwall in June, although we had not then met. Anthony was about to start training to be an accountant in the City. We did not envy them the weight of their packs but since there was nothing we could do about it, gave them some Imperial mints which were the only supplies we had on us and cantered off, feeling guiltily free and easy.

It was a particularly beautiful morning and the Way took us across country, and through a series of attractive villages. I was struck by the contrast between the simple hard-working peasant lives being led by the majority of the inhabitants, and both the signs of past grandeur and the incursions of modern progress. Many of the older and larger houses had imposing stone coats of arms on their façades, a particularly fine one in Zariquiegui, for example, with scallop-shells incorporated into the motif indicating the bearer's connection with the pilgrimage to Santiago. The churches usually seemed hugely out of proportion to the villages, towering over the huddled houses and capable of accommodating much larger congregations than exist today; this was so that in times of trouble the whole population of the town (and quite probably essential livestock as well) could take refuge in the nave. There were traces of long-gone castles, fortifications, towers on almost every hill. The farming, however, was mostly being conducted in a thoroughly modern manner, with giant tractors and combine harvesters creating great swathes of stubble across the rolling hills and leaving the strange big round bales scattered like giants' marbles. Not surprisingly, this machinery was kept in ugly modern sheds which intruded on the landscape.

A fairly stiff pull brought us to a high ridge, the Alto del Perdón, where looking back we could see the toiling figures of the two young Englishmen just starting the climb. Ahead, under the now cloudless sky from which the August sun was beginning to hammer at us, lay far below the villages through which we would be riding, and way beyond through the heat haze the distant wild mountains around Estella, which we hoped to reach before nightfall. This was no longer the lush pasture country of the foothills, but the start of the harsh, unforgiving Spanish heartland.

The descent was overgrown and very stony, leading through scrubby woods of evergreen oak, juniper and broom which rattled as we pushed through. Sheep grazed underneath, leaving a confusion of tracks. We came to a wire fence, over which a smart stile had been built for walkers, and we thought we were stuck. But there turned out to be a wire gate beside it, which we were able to open and lead the horses through. In gratitude Louella left two Imperial mints on the stile for Anthony and Julian. From then on it was fun to place more mints every mile or so in places where we hoped they would spot them. Eventually we left a note under a stone inviting them to supper in two days' time in Estella, where they should catch us up as we planned to rest the horses.

The soil was sticky in places after the rain and frogs leapt in shrinking puddles. The blackberries were just beginning to ripen and were to be a constant temptation to loiter. The blackthorn were heavy with dark purple sloes and both cowbells and church bells broke the silence from time to time.

In Uterga, a grand village with several fine decorated houses, we came on a begging gypsy woman on a donkey. It was old and thin and went slowly from house to house, resting its forehead on the wall by the front door while its mistress called out for alms in a quavering shriek. Our horses had been starting to flag in the heat, but at the sight of the donkey they became alarmed and highly skittish, so that we had trouble stopping them from bolting down the street. One or two locals, who had been leaning over their flower-decked balconies to scream back abuse at the gypsy, found this a fine diversion and cheered us on our way, calling 'Santiago!' as the Spanish used to do when charging into battle.

We were now approaching the point where the last of the other main routes to Santiago, the 'Somport' road from Arles, would join ours so that they would be all one for the rest of the Way. Strangely, we had already ridden part of that route when, on our way from the Camargue to Cornwall, we had passed through Montpellier and St Guilhem-le-Desert, one of the most significant places on any of the 'roads', having a relic of the True Cross in the church. It had been brought there by William, one of Charlemagne's generals, in 806, well before the cult of St James in Galicia had begun. When we were there we had barely heard of the pilgrimage to Santiago and it certainly never occurred to us that we might one day ride again to the west instead of to the north.

Now we backtracked for a couple of miles to the east on this equally well-marked trail to visit the captivating chapel of Eunate, one of the places we most wanted to see on the whole pilgrimage. The little 12th-century octagonal building standing alone in a corn-field was perfection.

Before setting out on the pilgrimage we neither of us knew much about Romanesque architecture. This was one of the first examples we met and whether or not it was a good example we were not equipped to tell, but for me it had everything. No one seems to know much about it, although the generally accepted theory is that it was a funerary chapel for pilgrims who were not going to make it all the way. It would be a good place to be buried. The setting is still virtually unspoiled in a basin of wooded hills, although one or two intrusive modern barns have sprouted in the distance. There is a most unusual external cloister, which surrounds and protects the small church from the outside world while providing somewhere for pilgrims to shelter.

The windows are made of alabaster, a translucent marble which, though opaque so that you cannot see through it, yet lets in a pleasant soft light. We were to see quite a number of churches lit this ancient way, but none illuminated a more satisfyingly symmetrical scene than the inside of the dome of Eunate. From each of the eight angles slender columns of unadorned square stone blocks rise to form a strong pattern on the roof and to meet and form a star. It is simple, uplifting and perfect.

While we were resting in a tiny patch of shade and allowing the horses to graze beside the cloister, a Guardia Civil car drove up and two grim-faced officers got out. I chattered nervously to them, guiltily suspecting as one does that we must have done something wrong. I showed them our letter from their Director-General, but they waved it away saying they knew all about us already. 'Where will you sleep tonight?' they asked. 'We hope to cover another 25 kilometres and reach Estella,' I replied. 'No,' they retorted. 'Our information is that you will only reach Puente La Reina today.' It was impressive to think that our progress was being so closely monitored, but I explained that the itinerary which they had been sent presented the most pessimistic picture and we hoped to improve on it greatly as our journey progressed. Still stern, and vetoing my request to photograph them with the horses, they saluted and left us.

In mid-afternoon the sun was at its most potent, searing the exposed skin of our faces and arms. Louella preferred to ride with her big black hat on her back, attached by the cord around her neck. Her hair was exactly the colour of the barley straw all round us, and drew admiring glances from men unused to seeing blondes. I worried about heat-stroke and advised her to wear her hat more, but she disliked having a sweaty forehead and in any case seemed not to suffer. In spite of her fair skin she never burned excessively either, although we both turned a darker shade of brown each day. She has a rare gift for concealing great resilience and fortitude behind a soft and pretty exterior which seems almost impervious to the elements and yet receives virtually no attention. Hairdressers, make-up, lotions and facials are not among her preoccupations and she has confessed to me that she is astonished by the time, effort and money so many of her girl-friends devote to such things. Yet, though accompanying me to some of the least hospitable hot places around the world, she exposes her skin to far more punishment than most.

And we were agreed that the plains of Spain in August were as hot and merciless as the Gobi desert, though without the sandstorms.

Puente La Reina is famed for the bridge which was built for pilgrims across the Río Arga in the 11th century by a queen. Which queen seems to be in doubt. Edwin Mullins firmly states that it was Queen Urraca, although she did not become queen of León-Castile until 1109. The invaluable *Guia del Peregrino* written by the late Don Elias Vœliñce of Cebreiro – we tore out the maps from one copy and carried them with us each day, while Joan kept a complete copy in the car for coordinating our rendezvous – says that it was Doña Mayor, the wife of Sancho the Great – or perhaps, on the other hand, it was Doña Estefania, her daughter-in-law. Another authority states it might have been Doña Mayor's grand-daughter who, if I have worked out the complicated Spanish genealogies of the time correctly, would have been Queen Urraca's mother.

What matters is that the delicate six-arched bridge is beautiful and now relieved of all but foot and animal traffic thanks to a by-pass. The town of Puente La Reina was in deep siesta as we rattled through the narrow cobbled streets to the Calle Mayor, the old pilgrim road, where the houses seemed to meet overhead, which led directly to the bridge. Mounting the bridge's raised span through the narrow western gate, we paused to look down at the river below and to consider how we could give the horses a drink. There had been no water at Eunate or since and we knew they were thirsty. The river looked dirty and unappetizing and there was no easy way down, so we enquired of a passing lady if there were a water-trough in town. She began to give us complicated directions, when a jolly stout gentleman in slippers bade us follow him to his house next to the bridge, where we dismounted and helped him to fill and carry outside a large red washing-up bowl, which the horses drank dry twice. A friendly crowd of locals awaking from their siestas gathered on their balconies and urged me on as I tried unsuccessfully to drain a final bowl myself.

The last 20 kilometres into Estella took us a good four hours. The track led us up a much steeper mountain than the one we had crossed in the morning and the horses were tired. Dropping down to skirt the perfect medieval town of Cirauqui, we joined the first of several stretches of Roman road which have survived the havoc of time, the weathered rows of large stones five paces apart worn by the tread of endless feet and hooves and separated by smaller cobbles. Often only one of the rows remained, but there was something about their permanence and the way they were set in the ground which identified them instantly for us as 'Roman'. The remains of a presumably contemporary humpbacked bridge spanned a narrow gorge. A wooden template had been constructed beneath it, either to hold it together or as the first stage in restoring it.

Beyond were more fine stone bridges lost in farming country where tiny green lanes separated vineyards, ploughed fields and abandoned scrub. By the time we had to join the main road and face the furious traffic for the last slow reach into Estella, we were all dropping with weariness. Then, as we finally crossed the Río Ega in the centre of town a small figure came running out, Louella reached down to swing him up behind her and he guided us proudly to our destination, chattering non-stop about the exciting time he, Joan and Jane had been having.

The horses were to spend two nights at their own home. Pablo Hermosa's stable overlooked the river and was entered from an alley, the Calle Curtidores or street of tanners. Opposite was the perfect Gothic doorway of Santo Sepulcro, surrounded by carvings of saints and with Biblical scenes above the door. Although not highly acclaimed in the guidebooks and hard to see due to the narrowness of the street, the thirteen concentric arches meeting in a row of musical angels are refreshing.

Inside the stables was a courtyard with walls from which hung every imaginable sort of ancient and modern tack and farm implements associated with horses. Yokes, bits, bridles, shoes, harrows, cruppers, rakes festooned every available space, the result of Pablo's father's obsession with collecting. A well with a pump stood in the middle and as soon as we had unsaddled them the horses were hosed down (which they manifestly enjoyed), given a good rub and led away to subterranean stables. There, in the security of familiar surroundings, we hoped that they would regain their strength for the serious travelling which lay ahead. Pablo himself was away with most of his horses taking a group of French and Belgian pilgrims on the last few stages into Santiago in time to greet the Pope. Even had we wanted to change one of our horses, and the opportunity to do so at this stage had been part of my deal with him, it would have been difficult since there was little left to choose from. In any case our pair matched each other so well, looked so good together and suited us so admirably that we had decided to risk Duque's sore developing and carry on with them.

It was almost dark as we made camp in a field above Estella belonging to Pablo. This was on the side of the Montejurra, which we had been able to see – rising up above the gorge in which Estella lies – from the Alto del Perdón that morning. This steep hill was the site of a major battle in the last century during one of the Carlist wars. Now it has a tunnel bored through it, which takes traffic around the town. We were high above this, behind the decaying church of Santa María and its convent, which had been converted into an old people's home.

Below us lay Estella la Bella, as it used to be called. The setting was beautiful and in the dusk the crass development which has spoiled much of the town was hidden. There was even a firework display to entertain us, the rockets exploding at about our level. For once we did not have to worry about the horses, snug in their stable down by the river.

DAY 4 Saturday 12th August   **REST DAY – ESTELLA**

We were woken by one of the stable-boys asking if we had seen a pony. The field in which we were camped formed a valley above the town. Corn had been harvested from it, but there was no fence between the stubble and the surrounding olive groves and scrub. The lad returned leading an adorable tiny, fat white stallion, which he tethered near our tents. It was a hot day, and by the time we had breakfasted and tidied up our camp the sun was beating down. I climbed to the top of the ridge above us to see the panorama of thickly wooded hills surrounding Estella with, far to the north, the limestone escarpments of the Sierra de Urbasa, like mountainous waves preparing to break on the plain. Looking down I gained a bird's-eye view of the town and, outside it, the ancient Benedictine monastery of Irache past which we would ride next morning. There is something about monasteries which draws the eye to them whatever the landscape in which they are set. Irache was founded in the 10th century and must once have worked and controlled most of the land around it. Today, the traces of old walled gardens, orchards and neat fields are being swallowed up to satisfy the expansive requirements of combine harvesters. But from far above it was possible to see their traces as well as to admire the Romanesque heart of the church, the fine apse and lofty dome, concealed from the visitor on the ground by all the later Renaissance additions.

Merlin, emerging naked from our tent in the mid-morning heat after a good lie-in, headed straight for the pony. After making friends, he climbed on its back and we photographed the pretty picture they made together. We all then went down into the town to shop for food and walk through the busy medieval streets, thronged with Saturday shoppers each seriously stocking up for a weekend influx of relatives. Laden with our own heavy shopping baskets we climbed up flights of steps to reach the church of St

Michael the Archangel, which I had read boasted a portal with some of the finest carvings in northern Spain. Frustratingly, the church was being restored and high fences laced with barbed wire thwarted our efforts to approach close enough to see anything.

We crossed back over the Río Ega by a lovely narrow single-arched bridge in the company of a flock of sheep. They slipped and stumbled on the steep cobbles which meet in a crest in the centre. The women following behind sensibly removed their shoes and crossed barefoot so as not to fall over and drop their precious packages. We had bought bread, local cheese, slices of indescribably succulent and delicious smoked ham and nectarines to go with it. On these, washed down with some good local red wine, we feasted with our backs against gnarled old olive trees in the grove above our camp. It was very pleasant in the shade and we planned to spend the afternoon reading and taking life easy for once. Merlin wandered off to have another chat with the little white pony. Idly we watched him offer it a piece of bread correctly placed flat on his outstretched palm, but instead of accepting the morsel it suddenly bared its teeth, grabbed Merlin by the shoulder and flung him in an arc over its back to hit the ground with an audible thump. In nightmare slow motion we raced down the hill towards him as he began to scream hysterically. Gathering him up in my arms, I knew at once that we must find a hospital. There was blood and mangled flesh visible on his neck and heaven knew what other injuries under his shirt. We carried him to the car thinking we would drive into town and ask the first person we met to give us directions. On a Saturday afternoon, it was going to take time. Then we thought of the old people's home, only a couple of hundred yards away. The nun at the reception desk saw the problem at once and directed us upstairs where, miraculously, there was a well-equipped clinic and an efficient nurse. She bathed the wound and examined it. Had the stallion's teeth met an inch to the left, they would have ripped Merlin's ear off; an inch to the right and they would have punctured his jugular. As it was, his skin was torn in a couple of places, dark blue and purple bruises were already forming, but there seemed to be no serious damage. We suggested an anti-tetanus injection but learning that he had had one in the last year, she assured us it was not necessary, treated the wounds with antiseptic, stuck on a big padded dressing and absolutely refused either payment or a donation to the home. 'We have no method of accepting money,' she said firmly.

We were all so grateful and relieved that it was not more serious that we felt frustrated at being able to do no more than repeat our thanks again and again. Merlin had stopped crying early on and concentrated instead on a healthy catharsis of vituperation against all horses and especially small white ones. When he had previously been stung by a wasp he had had much the same reaction, railing against all insects for a short while, then getting over it and showing no more fear of them thereafter. The same was to be the case with horses, fortunately. He slept beside us in the olive grove through the rest of the afternoon and when it was time to go down to our camp again, he walked past the pony happily, even giving it an insouciant pat.

Estella was a town invented in the 11th century as a settlement for the French, who were encouraged to remain there after making their pilgrimage to Santiago and so form a bastion against the Moors to the south. The Way is dotted with towns called Villafranca this or that which have the same origin. For centuries the need to keep the *Camino Francés* open served as the catalyst for expanding a Christian presence in Spain. The 12th-century Palace of the Kings of Navarra, said to be the oldest surviving secular building in Spain, lies at the heart of the old town on one side of a now peaceful square in which grow ancient pollarded plane trees. One of the columns of the palace has a famous capital showing Roland jousting with the giant Ferragut; it is a worn but lively carving in which it seems the giant is about to fall off his horse. Ferragut, or more properly in English Ferracute, meaning sharp iron, was a Saracen or Syrian descended from Goliath, reputed to be 36 feet high and with the strength of forty men. No spear could pierce his skin, but Roland slew him by stabbing him in the navel – his Achilles heel as it were – presumably after knocking him off his steed.

Opposite the palace, a long flight of steps leads up to the church of San Pedro de la Rua. As we climbed them a nightingale sang lustily from a bramble bush beside the wall. Being unfamiliar with nightingales, which occur in neither Cornwall nor Ireland, I was fascinated to find that this bird allowed me to come within a few feet and watch it warble its well-known song with open beak, while watching me from its little black eye. As a result I barely glanced at the richly decorated doorway to the church, but instead slipped inside where a service was being conducted to the accompaniment of more good singing. The Romanesque cloister of San Pedro contains one of the more endearing architectural jokes in that one of the groups of columns quite unexpectedly seems to have its legs crossed. The same trick is played in the late 11th-century cloisters in the monastery of Santo Domingo de Silos, but unless there is some significance I am unaware of, the purpose seems to be exclusively to entertain.

Day 5 Sunday 13th August ESTELLA TO VIANA

Jane was now to ride with us for three days. Up to this point she had been driving her car in convoy with Joan in ours, and with her fluent Spanish had been brilliant at showing what needed to be done as a support crew. Now she would leave her car in Estella and return in the truck which Pablo's boys would send to recover her horse. All they had for her was a rather cobby bay mare who they informed her was three months pregnant and should therefore be treated gently. Appropriately her name was Romera, meaning pilgrim. Concealing her disappointment at having to ride so plain a horse, Jane mounted the narrow military saddle which was the best they had left in the stables and joined us as we rode out of a largely still sleeping Sunday-morning Estella. Past the Palace of Kings we picked up the yellow arrows again, which took us along imaginatively routed trackways parallel to the main road for most of that day. We made good time along earthy country lanes where we could canter, through silent valleys where corn grew on the flat land and pine trees on the hillsides, while ruined castles added romance to unlikely crags.

As we entered Los Arcos at midday we overtook our first proper pilgrim, a Frenchman walking almost as fast as did the horses, so that we crept upon him very slowly. With his route map in a plastic case around his neck, sensible shorts, floppy hat and light pack, he had an air of professional determination which precluded light chat, although we were to meet and make friends later.

A long, narrow cobbled street led us into Los Arcos. It was again lined with balconies, out on to which people stepped at the sound of our horses' hooves – housewives wiping their hands on their aprons as they interrupted their cooking, children yelling to their parents to come and see the pretty horses, and all calling out greetings and good wishes to us. It is impossible to be inconspicuous on a horse and we found it best to respond in kind to the showmanship expected of us. Only when the young failed to recognize the scallop-shells on our shirts and hats and shouted, '*Ole, vaqueros,*' thinking we were cowboys, did I try to look stern and shout back, '*No vaqueros – peregrinos.*'

Outside the church a party of young Swiss pilgrims had gathered, looking tough and athletic in their walking gear. They crowded around our horses and were very friendly, but it turned out that they were not proper pilgrims but travelling in a minibus from which they walked selected stretches of the *Camino*. Among them, however, was a small dark girl who was altogether different. She stood out from the rest of the group, having something about her –

Setting off from the Monastery at Roncesvalles

Below: Louella and Jane overtaking a French pilgrim outside Los Arcos

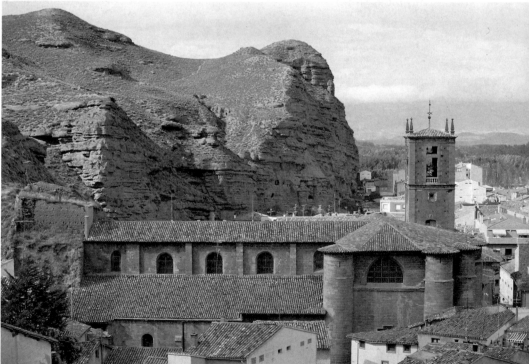

Top: The well-endowed equestrian statue of Santiago Matamoros in Logroño

Above: The Church of Santa Maria la Real in Najera which grows out of the red cliff with its miraculous cave

The remains of the Hospital of St Anthony near Hontanas looked fragile in the dawn light. *Inset:* The 12th Century green alabaster tomb of San Millan de la Cogolla in the Monastery at Suso

Top: Crossing a ruined Roman bridge between Puente la Reina and Estella

Above: The perfect Romanesque church at Frómista

a stillness, a strength, a sturdiness which they lacked for all their bravado. We had heard that there was a French girl who had walked alone all the way from Brittany and I asked her, '*Est-ce que vous êtes la jeune fille de Quimper?*' '*C'est moi,*' she answered modestly with eyes cast down, and we felt a surge of admiration for her courage. She never walked on Sundays and so was resting in this small village where she had met the group of students passing through.

Inside the church we were dazzled by a bewildering display of Spanish baroque at its most ornate. The whole nave seemed to be gilded, carved, painted, decorated so that one could practically hear the angelic trumpets. Two old ladies were fussing about in the aisle, arranging Madonna lilies in plain glass vases which contrasted starkly with the opulence around. There was about to be a funeral and they made it clear we should not linger. A priest from the village, who had lived for many years in Texas, had returned the week before to visit his family. Dying suddenly of a heart attack, he had come home for good.

One of the annoying and sad signs of progress was the result of a decision some bureaucrat must have made to upgrade and reorganize the road signs in this part of Spain. Solid stone markers made the stretches of paved road we had to follow less tedious as the kilometres could be counted off and, checking with maps and guides, we could at least tell exactly where we were. Sunk in the roadside vegetation and occasionally hard to see, these old milestones with their domed red tops gave a sense of permanence to the countryside. Now they were being grubbed out and flimsy narrow plastic or metal uprights were replacing them – not even at the same places but, according to some mysterious new formula, a kilometre or two further up or down the road. Apart from eyesores replacing entities, this meant that making rendezvous at kilometre signs – standard practice all over the Continent – was no longer a reliable matter since it depended on whether the old or new standard was being used. Outside Los Arcos we came on a graveyard of jumbled old-style milestones, their transitoriness emphasized by the Renaissance church tower behind them.

In Torres del Río we paused at another breathtaking octagonal church. Again it was the pattern of the vaulting inside the dome that was most striking. This time the columns did not meet in the middle, but instead were interrupted by rib vaulting whose columns swept past a central lantern in eight curves of perfect geometry to meet across the dome. Whereas the pattern at Eunate had felt familiar and simple, this design was clearly Moorish and so, though undeniably beautiful and clever, there was also something alien about it, at least in the supremely Christian context in which it was set. I was to have this feeling repeatedly on the pilgrimage as the wealth of the Islamic craftsmen's skills in stonework and design appeared in the churches we saw along the Way. Islam may have been superior to the Western world in all important respects at the time they were built, and it was only natural that the knowledge and art of that culture should have been incorporated into ecclesiastical as well as secular buildings; but Christian they were not, and they always jarred slightly. Just so would a Muslim feel, I imagine, seeing traces of the early Byzantine Christian church of Santa Sophia in Istanbul surviving its conversion to a mosque.

Our camp that night was beside a ruined house in a field just before Viana. There was thick grass and weeds for the horses to eat in the remains of the garden, and we were able to rig up a long rope between two trees so that they had plenty of room to graze. Lack of water was the only problem, so we led them to a small farm building visible a few hundred yards away, hoping that there might be a well. Instead we found two extremely cheerful families from the town enjoying their regular Sunday afternoon outing to their *finca* or country property. The dwelling was extremely simple, but there were tables and chairs under a pergola from which hung delicious grapes. One of the fathers was busy at the barbecue, on which mounds of spicy home-made sausages sizzled; best of all, there was a big concrete tank of water for irrigating the surrounding vegetable patches and orchards – the pretext for the whole set-up – and it had been converted into a deep swimming-pool. We were immediately made welcome and, after allowing the horses to drink their fill from buckets, invited to plunge into the pool. The water was cool and fresh, being pumped straight out of an artesian well, and nothing could have felt better after nearly eight hot hours in the saddle.

Jane, who really worked for the Ministry of Agriculture but was on secondment to the diplomatic service, had been telling us that she had recently written a report in which she had said, 'Scratch any Spaniard and you will find a farmer.' Nothing could have illustrated her point better than the existence of these *fincas* which seem to be an indispensable part of the lives of recently urbanized Spaniards. Instead of just having allotments to provide fresh home-grown vegetables, the plots are turned into pleasant refuges from the pressures of modern life, to which people are able to return to taste and re-establish contact with their origins each week. We were pressed to sample their sausages, to drink quantities of wine, to talk, sing and relax. As so often, Merlin was our best ambassador. With his blond curls, complete lack of shyness and robust approach to games he was soon the centre of an interested audience of children of assorted ages. Fortunately, there must have been a schoolbook or television

series about the Arthurian legend recently in Spain, for everywhere
we went his name was instantly recognized. 'Ay!' the children would
cry. 'Merlin el mágico!' 'No hablo español,' he stated stoutly, 'soy
Inglés.' and once that was sorted out it was a matter of only a few
moments before he was pursuing and being pursued around the
garden amid shrieks. The sun set behind the church tower of Viana,
silhouetted on a hill to our west, and still they pressed us to stay
on. The two families exuded weekend bonhomie and accepted us as
though we had known each other all our lives. It was hospitality at
its purest.

LA RIOJA

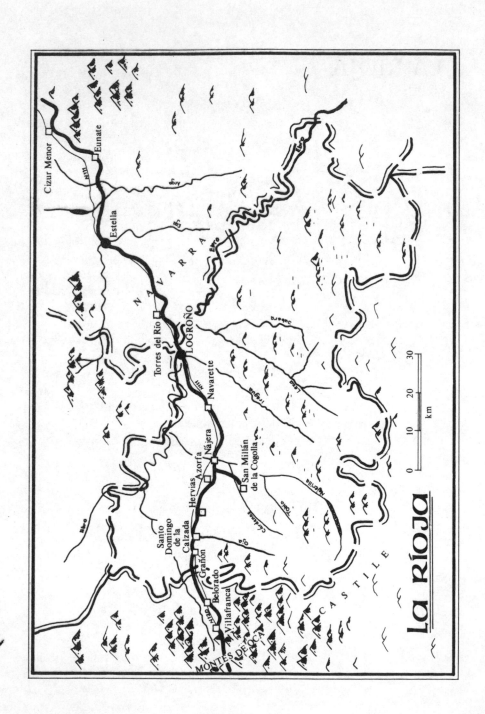

La Rioja

Duque had broken the scallop-shell on my *mosquero* by rubbing his forehead against the side of a church and so I had removed it from my bridle. Later I was to replace the real shell with a silver replica like those on our hats. Louella's was still intact and she had carefully laid down her bridle with our saddles against the garden wall. After we had fed and groomed the horses she walked over to collect it, to find that a long-tailed field-mouse was nibbling the horse-hair around the shell and had neatly reduced the contour by about half. It scurried off as she approached, but the damage was done. After that we always tried to hang our bridles out of reach of rodents.

As we entered Viana we passed the infelicitously named Restaurant Borgia, for this is where Cesare Borgia, brother of Lucrezia, is buried. Although notorious for their criminal political activities in Italy, they were the illegitimate children of a Spanish cardinal called Borja, who later became Pope Alexander VI. After he lost the French and Italian possessions, most of which he had acquired by foul means, Cesare escaped from prison and fled to Navarra of which his wife's brother was King. Five months later, in 1507, he was killed as he laid siege to Viana. Although at first he was buried inside the church of Santa María, a 19th-century bishop had Cesare's body exhumed and re-interred outside the porch so that those who despised his memory could step on his tombstone. We avoided letting our horses do so as we rode up to the church door, only to find it closed.

With far to go that day, we found a good drinking-trough in one of the attractive streets of the sleepy hill town and rode out of the province of Navarra and into La Rioja, famous for its wines. The capital, Logroño, lay just across the border on the Río Ebro, one of Spain's great rivers but now, we were sad to see as we rode over the stone bridge into the town, heavily polluted. Some friends of ours had been planning a journey by raft or small boat down the Ebro right across Spain to the Mediterranean, but we decided to dissuade them.

We rested in a leafy square where old men sat on stone benches and looked at us suspiciously before – almost, we felt, in spite of themselves – coming over to inspect the horses and tell us how it was in their youth when horse transport was the norm. The farmer inside every Spaniard, again!

Just south of Logroño is the site of the legendary battle which secured St James's reputation as a warrior and led to his becoming the patron saint of Spain. James and John, the sons of Zebedee, were fishermen of Galilee, 'plain, uncultured and poorly bred'. St James – known as the Great to distinguish him from St James the Less, the brother of Jesus – became the first of the apostles, being martyred by Herod Agrippa in A.D. 44 and so being the first of the twelve to enter heaven. The only suggestion of any warlike tendencies comes from the reference to the brothers as Boanerges or Sons of Thunder because they offered to bring fire down from heaven on some Samaritans for refusing to invite Jesus to stay.

But he turned, and rebuked them, and said, Ye know not what manner of spirits ye are of.

For the Son of man is not come to destroy men's lives, but to save them. And they went to another village.*

St James is known as a miracle worker, teacher and gentle healer, which is how most of the representations of the saint show him. By another of the coincidences which seem to have made our going on the pilgrimage to Santiago inevitable, for 25 years I have had a 17th-century wooden statue of St James in this guise as one of my most treasured possessions. The face is sad, ascetic, gentle and Christlike. Only the scallop shells on his breast reveal that it is St James.

According to the legend, which was not heard until the 12th century, a great battle took place at Clavijo in 844. Ramiro I of León and the Asturias confronted the vastly superior Moorish army of the Caliph of Córdoba, Abdurrahman (or 'Abd al-Rahman) II. He and his troops faced certain death, but during the night before the fight Ramiro dreamt that St James came to him in a vision and promised to help them win. Encouraged, they went bravely into battle shouting for the first time 'Santiago!' which has remained the Spanish war-cry to this day. St James duly appeared in the sky above the troops, dressed in shining armour and riding a white horse. He personally slew 60,000 of the enemy to bring about a great victory and the start of the Reconquest of Spain from the Moors. Although the whole story was, it seems, invented to justify the church of Compostela extracting tribute from the rest of Spain, the myth took hold and Santiago Matamoros (Killer of Moors) became the other image of the Saint. There could hardly be two more different characters incorporated together, but blended they were to provide just about every answer or hope sought by pilgrims for a thousand years as well as a unifying force for Spain. Within a single church we were to see both personalities of the saint regularly represented side by side, the gentle pilgrim with his staff, gourd bottle and scallop-shell next to the mighty warrior on his horse surrounded by the corpses of his enemies.

*St Luke's Gospel, chapter 9.

There was one of the latter sort in Logroño which we were determined not to miss, thanks to Edwin Mullins' vivid description of the monument on the Baroque façade of the church of Santiago el Real:

It was a colossal equestrian statue in stone of Santiago Matamoros with our hero thundering into the attack like Don Quixote in drag, sword flailing, his billowing robes destining him for certain to the fate of Isadora Duncan: he was mounted, what was more, on a stallion equipped with the most heroic genitals in all Spain, a sight to make any surviving Moor feel inadequate and run for cover.

We were not disappointed (see illustration section).

In Navarette we watered the horses at a fountain in the central square, where four stone carvings of Pegasus raised their left hooves in unison to strike water from Mount Helicon. Poets and the Muses are carried by a winged Pegasus when indulging in flights of fancy, so I felt entitled to sit on a bench lost in thought while Jane and Louella fended off the drunken attentions of a local who offered to marry each of them in turn but settled for a kiss instead. When a cross old lady pointed out that we were occupying the place where she and her cronies met each day in early afternoon, we went to see the priest and have our 'passports' stamped. He was very taken with Merlin, who had joined us with Joan and a picnic lunch, and gave him sweets and a scarf. Inside the church Merlin was, as usual, allowed to light candles for all his friends and relations. Quite often modern installations – where coins in a slot lit up electric bulbs – had replaced the much more satisfactory business with matches and boiling wax which gave a sense of adventure to the affair. 'If we light all the candles,' he said with the certainty of a four-year-old, 'we will see Jesus.' 'You see,' he announced unexpectedly on another occasion, 'Jesus died to save us. So now we are safe.' Since he could first talk he has had an invisible companion called Tod, who is extremely naughty and usually responsible for any accidents which may occur such as broken plates. At about this time he acquired a second friend called the Holy Ghost, also invisible but very, very good.

An endless afternoon through scorching featureless vineyards, the inedible bunches of sour grapes accentuating our thirst, brought us at last to Nájera, where we camped in a small courtyard next to the old bullring. The only attachment for the three horses to prevent them from stumbling over the guy-ropes or trampling on the tents was a big iron gate which bonged when they moved, so keeping us awake. They were restless, having only weeds to graze on and, in spite of being given an extra feed in the small hours, they never settled down. In the end Louella and I got up at 5 a.m. and took them down to the river where there was some good grass, and for a couple of hours at least they were happy.

DAY 7 Tuesday 15th August   NÁJERA TO SANTO DOMINGO

As the sun rose, the peace of the early morning in the sleeping town was broken by successive bangs from the countryside around. It was the 15th August, the Feast of the Assumption and a holiday in Spain, and Louella said they must be fireworks but I swore it was gunfire.

Across the stony Río Najerilla which runs through the town, redstone cliffs rose up fringed with a green blush of vegetation on top and honeycombed with caves. Many had doors, windows, galleries and flights of steps cut into the rock. It seems the river was prone to violent floods, and when these occurred the citizens of Nájera simply used to move into their second homes a few storeys up the cliff. We saw no sign of recent flooding and guessed that the general lowering of the water table all over Spain has probably reduced the incidence of floods everywhere.

Calling in briefly on the Franciscan fathers at the monastery of Santa María la Real to have our 'passports' stamped, we rode out of town, resolving to return the next day – which we planned to be a second one of rest for the horses – so that we could see the treasures. Passing the 15th-century church which grows straight out of the cliff and is exactly the same strange red, we followed the rough pilgrim Way up a cleft in the rock. Suddenly we were in quite different, unfamiliar country. Pine trees heavy with fir cones shaded the bare earth beside the dusty track and I half expected to smell the sea and find myself in Provence. Soon we were back in vineyards again, richer ones now, irrigated by a network of well-maintained concrete water-courses. We rode through Azorfa, which lived up to its reputation for hospitality, the people greeting and blessing us as we passed. Many of the houses had fine stone coats of arms on their façades, and it occurred to us that someone could have a lot of fun writing a picture essay which recorded all the arms to be seen along the Way. A wide, fertile valley was now spread out before us and we followed a maze of farm tracks which have cut and joined the old pilgrims' trail that once must have taken the shortest route but now has largely vanished. We were taking it very easy for the horses' sakes, never breaking out of a walk, enjoying the gentle pace and the colourful wild flowers which lined the tracks and canals. Even so we gradually overtook two figures, both of whom seemed to be walking in a most eccentric way, staggering from side to side and stopping frequently. They proved to be two pleasant German boys, one tall and rangy, one short and rather stout, who had left the French border on foot the day before we set out from Roncesvalles. Now their feet were in a bad way and they were about to give up and hitch-hike to Santiago instead. They did not seem too upset at the prospect of failing to earn their Compostelas.

We also discovered the source of all the bangs which did indeed prove to be gunfire, the result of the recent arrival of migratory quails from Africa and the start of their open season. The shooting seemed well-organized, one or two men following behind pointers which froze when they scented their game. Nothing else was shot, as I had feared when I had first heard the sound at dawn. One of the most unpleasant 'sporting' sights I ever saw was inside a car boot in Italy. The owner proudly opened it to reveal row upon row of goldfinches which he had shot in the nearby vineyards.

There seemed to be large numbers of quail about. They are proper edible game birds, delicious, and from then on we saw them on the menu everywhere. I asked one of the hunters whether he had had any partridges. He looked shocked and replied that the season for them did not begin until October.

Hervias is a small village just before Santo Domingo de la Calzada. The first building was a large rambling farmhouse, perhaps the remains of the old Hospital of Santa María de Valleota, once administered by the knights of Calatrava – one of the three Spanish orders of warrior knights committed to driving out the Moors. Surrounded by a well-tended garden, fruit trees and flowers with creepers climbing up its rough-stone walls, it felt welcoming even before we were espied by a woman hanging out washing from one of the balconies, and a man weeding the garden. Both spontaneously called to us, inviting us with unmistakable gestures to stop for a drink. Being unhurried for once, we rode into the courtyard and all enjoyed the great fuss made of us by the three generations of the family who poured out of various doors to greet us. The old grandfather pumped water from the well into buckets for the horses. His two daughters and their husbands, who worked in Madrid and were on holiday, helped us unsaddle and rub them down, while assorted grandchildren took it in turns to be allowed to sit on their backs. We were plied with wine, ham, olives, nuts, bread and cheese. All too soon we had to ride on, while they set off *en famille* to walk to the saint's day mass in the village. Such hospitality is all around in Spain, and had we taken twice as long over our pilgrimage we could have enjoyed it every day.

Riding into Santo Domingo de la Calzada felt natural, since the pilgrim Way runs straight through the town along a narrow street away from most traffic and thronged, as we approached the cathedral, with tourists and pilgrims who had come by bus, car or bicycle. We were objects of gratifying interest and admiration. There was even a parador, one of the luxurious Spanish state-owned hotels, often converted castles but in this case the original 11th-century hermitage of Saint Dominic of the Causeway himself, which he rebuilt as a hospital before his death in 1109 at the age of ninety. He was famed as a builder, especially of bridges and roads across difficult country which he constructed in order to help pilgrims on their way. The cathedral, which was built over his tomb, was started in 1158 and finished in 1180. It is one of the earliest largely Gothic buildings in Spain, the French influence brought by the early pilgrims. Before visiting it, we had to find somewhere for our horses to stay. While Louella and Jane held the horses in the square, providing the crowd of tourists with an unusual and appropriate foreground for their pictures of the cathedral, I went into the parador and asked the manager his advice. After some thought, and perhaps to remove my dusty and unsuitable presence from his elegant foyer, he revealed that the owner of a rival establishment, the Corregidor, owned horses and might be able to help us. Attached to that hotel was a smart restaurant called El Peregrino, in front of which was a newly seeded lawn whose irrigated grass had shot up 6–8 inches and was badly in need of mowing. The sight of such lushness after the parched countryside with its desiccated weeds was irresistible and, much to Jane's diplomatic horror, I turned the horses in through the gateway and let them start grazing. We made sure they did not tread on the grass but only ate as fast as possible what they could reach from the path. Superior clients of the restaurant, leaving at 5 o'clock in the afternoon after a good late lunch, picked their way past us with their noses in the air, but the horses showed admirable restraint, or perhaps were just too busy, and there was nothing for them to step in. We got away with it for some twenty minutes before an apoplectic manager arrived and screamed at us to leave. I tried to reason with him. 'Look,' I said, 'they have done no damage; in fact, think how much less mowing will now be necessary. And anyway, they are pilgrims like us and so you should be pleased to feed them.' But he was lacking in any sense of humour and shooed us out like vagabonds. Partly out of bravado at this treatment and partly because we felt we deserved a treat, we then checked in to the hotel, making it quite impossible for the owner (when he eventually turned up) not to help us over the matter of the horses. He had a farm outside the town, back along the way we had come, to which I rode with his young nephew on Guadalquivir to show the way, while Louella settled into our very comfortable accommodation.

Jane meanwhile had arranged to be collected by Pablo's son in the truck and so, after several celebratory drinks in the hotel bar, she and Romera departed. It had been fun and invaluably instructive having her with us, as her knowledge of Spain, its people and language was huge and her advice and example had saved us endless complications. Merlin, in particular, would miss her as they had become great friends. He had enjoyed having an ally who did not feel responsible for him and so was not always telling him what to do.

Perhaps because of this, he was being particularly enchanting at this stage. With his fair hair and skin he had learned that he could break the thickest Spanish ice instantly and he now set about doing so in the hotel, racing around in an ecstacy of joy at feeling carpet under his bare feet and having a lift to play with. In northern Europe he would have been considered a darned nuisance and quickly suppressed, but the staff indulged him outrageously and, like Eloïse in the children's story books, he soon had the whole place under his thumb. By then his feet were so tough that he could run flat out across stony ground, virtually ignoring thistles and thorns. Covered in small scratches and cuts, not to mention the scar from the pony bite healing on his neck, his skin browner each day, he wore the minimum of clothes and through being scrubbed regularly tended to look quite clean. Perhaps because we left and rejoined him each day, he was being exceptionally loving towards us, racing to greet us each evening and spontaneously reaching up to kiss his mother's hand, a self-taught gesture which astonished and delighted the Spanish. A furious temper lay not far below the surface if he was thwarted, but Joan was brilliant at pre-empting that, her patience extraordinary as they played elaborate games together, did their exercises, set up and took down our camps.

The Hotel Corregidor was named after the 12th-century judge who inadvertently provided the town of Santo Domingo de la Calzada with its most popular tourist attraction. According to the local legend, a young French pilgrim was falsely accused of theft and hanged. His distraught parents prayed to Saint Dominic and Saint James and were rewarded by hearing their son speak from the gallows. Seeking out the judge, the parents told him the unlikely story as the great man was just sitting down to dinner. Annoyed at being disturbed, he retorted that the criminal was no more alive than the cock and hen he had just roasted. At that the birds jumped up on to the table, the cock crowed . . . and the boy was released. Ever since, a pair of chickens has been kept alive in a glass-fronted henhouse in the cathedral, to the delight of tourists seeking something novel. The Lake poet and close friend of Coleridge, Robert Southey, wrote a poem describing the legend. It is pretty dreadful stuff, but interesting in the variety of other legends about St James included in the poem. Two verses will give the general flavour:

> And how he used to fight the Moors
>   Upon a milk-white charger:
> Large tales of him the Spaniards tell,
>   Munchausen tells no larger.

> But in their cause of latter years
>   He has not been so hearty;

> For that he never struck a stroke is plain,
> When our Duke, in many a hard campaign,
> Beat the French armies out of Spain,
>   And conquer'd Buonaparte.

When the boy is found to be alive, he is made to say:

> 'Mother,' said he, 'I am glad you're return'd,
> It is time I should now be released:
> Though I cannot complain that I'm tired,
> And my neck does not ache in the least.'*

He was Poet Laureate when he wrote this!

Such frivolous diversions are really not necessary inside the church, where the soaring stonework and breathtaking vaulting above seemed literally to lift one towards heaven.

As we craned our necks and speculated in whispers as to how such an ambitious and delicate architectural masterpiece could have been created without any of the cranes and lifts which would be taken for granted as indispensable today, Merlin provided his own solution to the problem. 'They must have had Spiderman suits,' he told us. He especially liked that church as, in addition to the chickens, there was a delayed light switch in Saint Dominic's crypt which he could just reach. As each new group of visitors made their way down the steps to see the mausoleum, he proudly turned it on to illuminate the scene for them. Delightful carvings of the saint encouraging his disciples to build bridges, to cut and shape blocks of stone surround the tomb, and he comes across as a really saintly character with an individual personality revealed in his personal concern for each stage of the job being completed.

Another vast and vulgar gilded altarpiece fills the apse. Once the shocking contrast between the austerity and purity of line of the body of the church and the exuberence of these retables had been reconciled, I began to enjoy them for what they were – extraordinary pieces of sculpture. This one was produced by one of Spain's most

* See Appendix 4.

brilliant sculptors, Damian Forment, shortly before he died, and is full of colourful and lively Bible stories. Coated in gold leaf and painted over, the paint is then scratched away to create the dazzling highlighting.

After the hardness, asceticism and indeed pain of a week in the saddle, the contrast of a hot, soapy bath and a clean bed was peculiarly enjoyable. It has always been my article of faith that neither self-indulgent creature comforts nor the austerity which placates the puritan in me are satisfactory without the contrast of the other. While travelling, my innate mild manic-depression is enhanced. I become unreasonable and angry with myself much more than with my travelling companions, and feel depths of fury and frustration which seldom hit me at home. There the depressions are more insidious, less sudden. Travelling, the happy mania of joy at the beauty, the excitement, the sense of achievement, the closeness with my companions far outweigh, for me at least, the disadvantages. I hope they do for the others, too, and that they forgive me my irritability.

As always when travelling it is the insecurity which stimulates, and this is especially strong when horses and a young child are both involved. Disasters, which wait to strike at every moment during any journey, are daily much closer now and this keeps us on our toes.

DAY 8 Wednesday 16th August   REST DAY

As we breakfasted late off good china on the white linen tablecloths of the hotel restaurant, we could look onto the pilgrim's Way outside the window. Into view strode the Frenchman we had met three days before outside Los Arcos, head down below his back-pack and legs pumping rhythmically. We called to him, begging him to join us for coffee and croissants, while explaining rather shamefacedly that we were spoiling ourselves. He smilingly declined, saying that he must press on and, for once on the other side of the fence, we did not try to persuade him.

The monastery of San Millán de la Cogolla lies off the main Way and so now we drove there; there are in fact two monasteries, one very early and one much later. The saint is supposed to have lived in the cold wet cave of Suso, meaning 'above', for 101 years from 473 to 574, though he must have had a remarkable constitution to do so. Moisture seeped from the damp red rock, and even in mid-

August it was a chilly place. The chapel was built into the living rock by the Visigoths, the western branch of the Germanic people who occupied Roman Spain at the end of the 4th century and were themselves expelled by the Moors in 711. In it is a great and beautiful treasure carved in the 12th century out of a huge solid block of pale green alabaster. It is the saint's tomb with his lifesized body carved sleeping on top, surrounded by dwarf devotional figures of monks and, apparently, nuns who gaze up at him with rapt adoration and hold out objects like books and boxes associated with his life. It is a wonderfully lively scene, full of interest and action. Even the obligatory dog is not asleep under his feet but straining at its leash on the tomb's side. There is a sense that the initiative of the saint is being carried on through the centuries. And so it was. Saint Dominic of the Causeway offered himself as a young man to the monastery some 500 years after the saint's death and, when rejected, went off and started building bridges, perhaps to prove that he could do it too. Meanwhile a thriving cult grew up around San Millán, rivalling for a time that of Saint James himself. Legends developed that he too was to be seen on a white horse at the head of armies fighting the Moors. He also gave his name to the St Emilion region of Bordeaux where some of the world's greatest clarets are produced, notably Château Cheval Blanc, which rounds off his story nicely as perhaps it refers in some forgotten way to the saint's white charger.

From Suso there is a fine view across the deep fertile Cardenas valley to the hills opposite, over which the holm oak woods are draped like a continuous blanket. Snug in the valley lie the Renaissance buildings of the monastery of Yuso ('below') built originally in 1053 by the Benedictines, whose founder was a contemporary of San Millán. St Benedict's Rule included manual work on the land, so that his followers became the first 'green' Christians, practising good husbandry and seeking self-sufficiency from a world which they were taught not to abuse. Sadly there are all too few other threads in the Christian tradition which continued this respect for nature. Instead there has been – throughout the Middle Ages and since – a concentration on the redemption of mankind and a rejection of the natural world. This is now changing, I believe.

A Benedictine nun, St Hildegard of Bingen (1098–1179), was one who expressed her Order's views powerfully in her poetry, her morality play and her music. Today she is increasingly regarded as one of the most vivid and original voices from the past to evoke a green philosophy. Her writings are full of a robust, almost physical love of the earth.

The Earth is at the same time mother. She is the mother of all, for contained in her are the seeds of all. The Earth of humankind contains all moistness, all verdancy, all germinating power. It is in so many ways fruitful.*

In the beginning all creatures were green, flowers bloomed in their midst, afterwards greeness descended.

St Francis of Assisi (1181–1226) went on the pilgrimage to Santiago himself. Recent studies of his writings, too, have shown the relevance of his inspiration to modern concerns about the relationship between human beings and the rest of creation. His *Canticle of Brother Sun*† has been called the highest poetic expression of an original Christian thinker. In it and in his other writings he shows how man and nature can be reconciled, can live lightly on the earth.

The Benedictines remained at Yuso until 1833. Now a handful of Augustinians rattle around the echoing buildings and cloisters, taking groups of tourists in the morning and afternoon. It is a grand setting, crying out for occupation and activity. The sight which cheered me most was a glimpse into the extensive vegetable garden, which looked well tended and gave a momentary impression of hard-working monks dutifully hoeing their rows and digging till they gently perspired.

On the drive back to see Nájera properly, we stopped to inspect an attractive little stone building, shaped exactly like an old-fashioned beehive, of the kind sometimes made into yellow china honeypots. There was a low entrance and the domed interior was blackened with soot. Two Lesser Horseshoe bats looked down and twitched with alarm as I poked my head in, but there was no clue as to the building's purpose. It seemed much too fine to be a simple shepherd's shelter, but nor did it appear to be a kiln. Perhaps someone will enlighten me one day.

The interior of Santa María La Real in Nájera led us underground again, as the church does indeed grow out of the red cliffs at its western end. Dozens of carved tombs here too, as this was the pantheon or burial place of local royalty in the 11th and 12th centuries, the most touching and delicate being that of Doña Blanca, who died in childbirth and is surrounded by weeping figures and biblical scenes. Behind the sarcophagi is a cold grotto in the rock guarded by the kneeling figures of King Garcia of Navarra, son of Sancho the Great and his Queen Estefania of Barcelona. The king was out hunting in 1044 and he released his falcon after a dove; since the adjoining monastery was to become one of the first and greatest pilgrim refuges along the Way, we must assume it was a peregrine. Hawk and prey disappeared into a cave in the cliff; when the king went in he found them both crouched peacefully together

* McDonagh, Sean, *To Care for the Earth*, p. 135.
† See Appendix 5.

in front of a statue of the Virgin, which caused him to have the church built. The painted wooden statue there now is 13th-century and still revered for its miraculous powers. Fresh white carnations and Madonna lilies were arranged in vases at its feet. The Virgin herself, gentle-faced, right hand raised in benediction, emanates tranquillity, but the infant Jesus, held in her left hand, is a disappointing small black pin-headed puppet.

It was in the 16th-century Knight's Cloister that I first became excited by the wonderful carvings of medieval life to be found on the capitals there and in many subsequent cloisters. Above was the decorative plateresque tracery of stonework between the arches, casting pretty shadows on the paving stones. Known as 'plateresque' because of its detail and similarity to the work of silversmiths, this stonework is as rich and delicate as any to be found in Europe. Paradoxically, it was both influenced by the exuberance of the art of the departing Moors and stimulated by the influx of quantities of Aztec and Inca silver from the New World. Below, unmistakable among the Bible stories squeezed around the top of each column were glimpses of how it really was for farmers, soldiers and pilgrims, for what other models than those around him could the sculptor have drawn on? Animals real and imaginary peered out of frozen foliage, teeth bared, biting, pursuing. Birds preened and stretched their wings, cherubs played with wolves, saints gazed heavenward in rapture. A rider lay propped against a tree holding his horse's reins and considering whether to pluck a handy bunch of grapes. Strangely, the horse had cloven feet. I found it hard to tear myself away.

Towards evening, as gusts of wind whipped up paper and women's skirts in the narrow streets, heralding a violent rainstorm, we all climbed up the cliff to try to visit some of the domestic caves, but they were locked. Below us the pantile roofs of the old town blended perfectly with the surrounding rock and soil, while exactly on our level two storks tended their colossal nest perched on the very top of a church tower and fed invisible young. And so back through sunset and squalls, past a landscape where the field patterns made tartan stripes on the hills, distant cloudbursts brought shafts of sunlight down from heaven and clumps of green woodland tempted us to camp again.

CASTILE

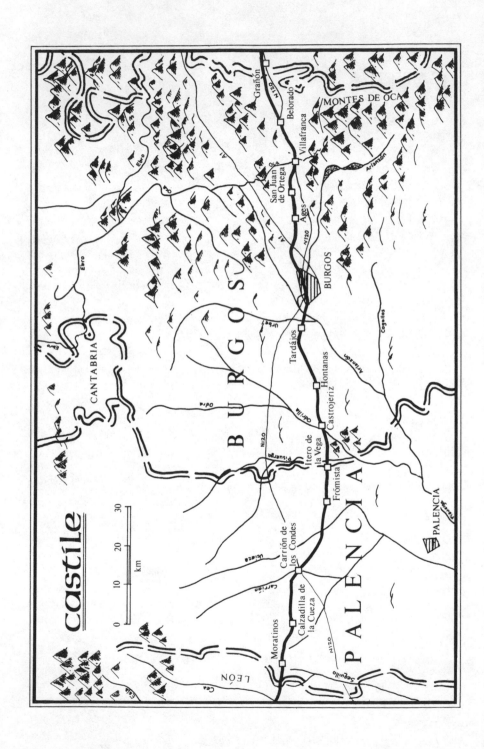

Wine-growing La Rioja, which we were about to leave, takes its name from the Río Oja, which runs past Santo Domingo de la Calzada. The wide river bed was dry and as we crossed by the main road bridge we looked down on a gypsy encampment. A pretty, very dark girl suckled a baby and watched over a dozen urchins who played among the stones. Bedding and clothes were spread out in wide circle around her tent and cart, to which an old horse was tied. It seemed as though a temporary territorial statement was being made; this was their space and for the time being it was not to be invaded. There was no sign of any other adults or older children and we suspected they were out in the town through which we had just ridden for the second time, begging and fleecing the tourists as they emerged from their buses and headed for the chickens in the church.

At Grañón we were welcomed with special enthusiasm. It is a small and pretty place with a fine 14th-century church, a good main street lined with once noble houses, and a strong impression of having seen better times. Once Grañón considered itself equal if not superior to Santo Domingo across the river, but the road bypassed the town taking with it the bulk of pilgrim traffic. Only occasional footsloggers pass through now, and even they are likely to lose the traces of the old *camino* which have disappeared under the plough and the new scale of farming. On our horses we were able to take short cuts, heading straight across country for places we wished to visit. In the main square old ladies in black jostled for position around the travelling greengrocer, while we were surrounded by friendly children who petted the horses, students who earnestly made notes about our route for some school project, and the mayor who came out of his office to stamp our 'passports'.

Louella started to queue, as we fancied the idea of some fruit for our thirst, but the old ladies (having, we supposed, lost the village shop) were making the most of the opportunity to haggle and pick over the goods and we, of course, had far to go. 'How about some pears for two poor pilgrims?' I called over the heads of the crowd to the stall-holder. He laughed and threw me two, refusing the payment I pressed on him – I was embarrassed that my Spanish was inadequate to explain the difference between poor, meaning hot and thirsty, as opposed to an inability to pay. The pears were sweet and juicy, banishing for a time the tedium of our antlike pace beneath the blazing sun. And now that we were only two we did make better speed, breaking into a canter spontaneously when conditions were right, without the worry of Jane's pregnant mare, our pair being well matched and even showing a trace of competitiveness when fresh in the morning.

To try to spare Duque's constantly threatening saddle-sore I had switched saddles with Jane and was now riding on Pablo's narrow, hard but much lighter military saddle, known as a Maclean, while she had enjoyed my luxurious Camargue one on Romera. This had worked, so I now packed my saddle away in the car for the rest of the journey – to Duque's if not my own greater comfort.

We skirted the main road with its urgent roaring trucks, its smells, danger and litter, passing through one village after another where the 20th century – audible, intrusive and sometimes only yards away – seemed to be consciously ignored. Milk churns stood outside many houses and it took us a while to realize that in these the ground floor was occupied by milch cows while the family lived above, with hay and corn stored under the roof. The fountains, for which we would always enquire for the horses' sakes, were usually well maintained and used as cattle troughs instead of being dry or full of litter as was too often the case in the larger towns. Old people sat in doorways, sometimes sewing or cleaning vegetables but more often doing nothing.

In Belorado, a prosperous little town with a thriving industry manufacturing and marketing leather goods, we unsaddled the horses in the shady green in front of the church of Santa María, where we were pestered by bumptious children on bicycles who bombarded us with questions without listening to the answers. I bought a couple of *bocadillos de jamón*, the wafer-thin freshly-cut slices of succulent smoked ham bursting from the long crisp rolls – to translate this as a ham sandwich would be simply misleading – and we munched happily under the trees, the children having moved on. The church had both Santiagos, Matamoros and pilgrim in it, and being on the edge of the town was a sleepy pleasant place. It was always an effort to get going again in the middle of the afternoon.

Both Belorado and Villafranca Montes de Oca, which we reached that evening, were settled by French pilgrims in the 12th century, and French would have been spoken for 200 or 300 years thereafter, but there is little or no trace of it now. Joan had persuaded the archaeologists working on the ruined Royal Pilgrims' Hospital of St Anthony that we should be allowed to camp there rather than stay in the refuge down in the village. The main attraction of this was that a big field with a hedge all around it (something we had not seen since leaving Basque country) lay next to the hospital. Having only recently been harvested, it had fresh straw, grass around the verges and even uncut patches for the horses to gorge themselves on. We only hoped that they would not make themselves ill, but it would be very good for them to have a night of freedom to graze their fill after being stabled outside Santo Domingo for two nights.

Merlin found the location completely satisfactory as there was a bell over the gateway with a convenient rope, on which he was allowed to swing and announce our arrival. To the archaeologists' horror, we chose to sleep in the porch of the abandoned church. They urged us to use one of the rooms they were excavating, where we would at least be protected from the night air, but we could see that there was a good flat surface under the vaulted roof at the top of the steps next to which we could park the car. With our beds spread out up there we would get the best of both worlds, shelter from possible rain and a view of the stars without having to put up the tents. It was a most romantic setting for sleep, and despite a few visits from curious dogs and old ladies, we slept well.

DAY 10 Friday 18th August
VILLAFRANCA TO TARDÁJOS (BURGOS)

There is nothing so convenient as a flight of church steps for getting dressed and breakfasting. Each level provided a solid surface for the small gas cooker, mugs of coffee, cornflakes, toast and jam. There was even a convenient shelf down the side for clothes, torches and the like. It made a change not to be sitting on dew-damp grass in an uneven field where everything tended to fall over. Leading the visibly fatter horses back between the trenches and tapes of the still sleeping professors, we were up and away in no time. The Montes de Oca, through which we now rode, were one of the most notorious stretches of the Way. Thickly wooded and infested with bandits and wolves, it was a place through which to hurry and pray.

There are still a few wolves in the mountains of northern Spain. They are shy and persecuted, representing no danger to man and there may even be more than people are generally aware of, being so well hidden and migratory that they are hardly ever seen. I heard an extraordinary story about one mammal researcher who was tracking down records of sightings of wolves on the outskirts of Paris; they must have been travelling between the nearest known populations in Germany and Spain along ancient routes which their instincts still told them to follow. If this story is true, then the power of an urge which will attract an animal several thousand miles across hostile country with all the dangers posed by man, dogs and traffic, defies the imagination.

We heard and saw no wolves, but the woods were wild and peaceful in the cold misty morning as we climbed up through oaks past hoopoes and larkspur to reach heather, juniper and dwarf conifers. Lichen hung thick in festoons from the trees, a sure sign of clean, unpolluted air and an indication that there was not much industry between us and the Atlantic. Also from now on we began to see ragwort, a kind of groundsel, known in Spain as St James's grass. Its Latin name is *Senecio Jacobaea* and it is a particularly noxious and invasive yellow weed about 2 feet high. I remember it being called 'Stinking Willie' as a child during the war, and being told by my mother that it was against the law to let it grow so that I must always pull up any I saw. Like feeling guilty about eating in the street (a heinous crime when I was at school), the sight of ragwort always makes me think I should do something about it. It is strange that a plant should have such an effect, but stranger still that research has shown its alkaloids to be associated with liver cancer.

We dropped steeply down from the watershed to the remains of the hermitage of Valdefuentes, like an oasis in the constant woodland. Stumbling upon it must have gladdened the hearts of many lost and frightened pilgrims in the past. Today the main road runs past and there are picnic tables. As we grazed the horses beside the chapel, there was a roar of motors and a convoy of twenty Guardia Civil motorcyclists sped past in tight formation escorting two black limousines. We wondered what was up. Behind them came a bearded pilgrim pushing a small cart loaded with his possessions. We already knew of each other's existence through the bush telegraph which informs all pilgrims about others on the Way, and now we introduced ourselves and began to compare notes. He was Belgian and had walked all the way from his home. When Louella asked him why he was making the pilgrimage, he replied that he had worked as a schoolteacher for forty years and been married for thirty-five of them. On retirement he found himself suddenly at home with a wife to whom he had nothing to say. Following the Way of St James, he wrote to her each day and she to him at *postes restantes*. It was, he said, like a honeymoon all over again and they were in love once more.

Following wide forestry tracks and firebreaks between plantations of pine woods, we began to catch sight of dusty golden plains ahead. Rising out of the last of the woodland was the distinctive church tower of San Juan de Ortega showing the profile of its three bells. I had been to San Juan during my earlier visit in May and was looking forward to returning and meeting again the parish priest

Padre José María Alonso, who looks after the church and monastery virtually single-handed. A scattered hamlet of small farms surrounds the cluster of ecclesiastical buildings, and it is a place of great beauty and peace. The founder saint was a disciple of Santo Domingo de la Calzada, and as great a builder of bridges and causeways for the benefit of pilgrims. Of all the refuges we saw along the Way, San Juan de Ortega stays in my memory as the one best designed to bring comfort to the weary traveller. The mellow stone and absence of any sign of the 20th century unless a car has made its way down from the main road; the silence and lack of movement, except for a few pecking chickens; the rough track by which we approached from the east . . . all contributed to the sense of timelessness.

The priest, however, was away; in Santiago, we were told by his housekeeper, to see El Papá. We had better hurry if we were going to arrive in time, as he would be there tomorrow. This was a joke with which we were very familiar, since those we passed had often urged us on with the same words, assuming that we – like so many others over the preceding weeks – were on our way to see the Pope. With 500 kilometres still to go, it would of course only be possible to do so in a fast car – which suddenly explained the police motor-cycles. With a million or so pilgrims flooding into Santiago over the weekend, every policeman who could be spared was being rushed there.

Padre José María had shown me the ambitious restoration work he was having done on the extremely dilapidated cloister and monastery quarters, more as an act of faith than because he had yet raised the money. But, he told me, with all the interest in the pilgrimage arising from the Pope's visit, he had high hopes that things would now begin to look up. I should have guessed that he would have ensured he was near the action at such an important moment.

Inside the church we were able to admire the saint's intricately carved tomb with episodes from his life depicted around the sides. Surviving a shipwreck on his return from a pilgrimage to the Holy Land, he had vowed to build a hospital for pilgrims in the wild country he came from, where nettles (*ortigas*) made life for the barefoot traveller even harder. This tomb is a later Gothic addition, being 15th century. Like Santo Domingo de la Calzada, he is por-trayed as a kindly man blessing animals and children, while building for the comfort of all.

Around the capitals of the original Romanesque columns are tender, flowing carvings of scenes from the Bible, which I found very touching. In particular there is a Nativity in which the infant Jesus in his crib is carried above the sleeping Mary by an angel, while cattle rest their muzzles on his swaddling clothes between wooden buckets hanging from a beam. All the figures around are gentle and compassionate. The 12th-century builder so designed the church that a single shaft of sunlight strikes these figures alone just twice a year on the spring and autumn equinoxes, the 21st March and the 23rd September. At precisely seven minutes past five in the evening they are illuminated in the surrounding darkness of the church interior by the soft glow of a gleam which has passed through the alabaster of a strategically placed slit window.

Although we were now not far from Burgos, the capital of Castile, the Way ran across country right to the outskirts of the town through some of the pleasantest landscape imaginable. After the final thinning edges of the pine woods, where patches of shade and sunshine, wild-flowers and heathland alternated, we came out once more on to a valley of rich farmland where the stubble of the recently harvested barley stretched in all directions. There below us lay Ages, a perfect small village without a single modern building, looking much as it must have done for 500 years. Beyond it was the last barren ridge of hill which we must cross to see Burgos. Scarlet poppies enlivened the uncultivated headlands, mixed with brightly coloured flowering thistles, purple and yellow, as well as teasels, which are now rarely seen in English fields. They have large prickly burrs on their flower-heads, which used to be used for teasing cloth and raising a nap on the surface, thus giving us teasing as a word for worrying something or someone.

We walked and led the horses over the stony, scrubby ridge. By now they would follow us and showed no desire to run away, so that we could leave them free when we stopped to rest and let them graze on whatever was available. The open country continued even after we had crossed the autopista which bypasses Burgos, and we were still able to canter over the fields from time to time. In this way we overtook the little French girl from Quimper, walking now with a young Frenchman from the group in Los Arcos. We talked for a time, finding that our walking speeds matched each other almost exactly. We were impressed by the distances they covered each day, but they agreed that the freedom given by horses would add to the enjoyment.

Then we reached the horrible suburbs of Burgos and had to follow the dangerous main road into town, running the gauntlets of silly youths who shouted at the horses from café tables and speeding lorries which flashed past with inches to spare. Driving in a car the outskirts of a town are often barely noticed unless one gets lost in them, but on a horse they seem endless. Moreover, faulty street map-reading can easily add an extra half-hour or so instead of simply a frustrating few minutes. Asking the way is not always as easy as it sounds either, since most people cannot understand that mounted it is much quicker to go direct through little back streets than around by the new dual carriageway as one would in a car.

At last we reached the narrow old cobbled lanes around the cathedral and suddenly came out on a terrace almost on a level with the 'poetry in stone' of the spires, which Philip II of Spain called 'the work of angels'. It is an incredible sight, the stonework fretted, pierced, almost teased into airy traceries against the sky. But at that moment we found it overpowering, tired as we were and worried about our horses and the distance we still had to travel before nightfall. I could only remember Edwin Mullins' cricketing simile of the effect Spain had had on the refined Gothic architecture of France and Germany, bringing their enthusiasm to a climax in Burgos. The Spaniards, he writes, 'seized on Gothic in much the way the Barbadians and Trinidadians seized upon our gentle English summer games with a gusto that soon wrought a transformation inconceivable to its originators'. It was all too much for us to appreciate and so, feeling rather guilty at not spending longer, we rode on, resolving to return when we were feeling stronger.

As we were to find out the next day the interior of the cathedral does demand a strong stomach, at least in the Chapel of the Holy Christ where a much venerated effigy of Christ on the cross is covered in lifelike skin and hair, with a great wound gaping in the neck and apparent sores on the naked body. The chapel was full of devotees, however, and usually is very well attended.

On the edge of the town we watered the horses in the river below the Malatos Bridge and then, as the light faded and our spirits dropped, we urged on ourselves and our weary mounts for more than two hours until we reached Tardájos, the first village beyond the suburbs, where we had arranged to meet Joan and Merlin. Joan had done very well, getting permission for us to sleep on the floor in the school, which we had to ourselves, while the horses could spend the night in the playground. Our knees, backs, shoulders, necks and ankles all ached and we felt we could not go another yard, so it was quite a relief not to be setting up camp. The only problem was that there was nothing for the horses to eat in the playground; they would need more than their nosebags of corn and so I set off, feeling a bit like a beggar seeking alms, to see if I could track down some hay in the village. Everyone was kind and helpful, directing me from one farmer's barn to another, but those who were in had no hay, while those whom we had been assured would have some were out. At last I met a kind man with a weatherbeaten face and a handshake like picking up a lobster, who said he could solve my problem. 'First, however,' he said, 'you must come and have a drink with me.'

Thinking that this would at least give me a chance to buy him a couple in a bar, I followed him. However, instead of heading towards the lights of the village square, he led me out into the countryside where it was pitch-dark and we stumbled together across stony ground and up a hill. By now I was past caring what fate lay in store for me, and anyway it would have been much too rude to say that I was tired and wanted to go home and so we trudged on in silence. At last we came to a small wooden door set into the hillside, which – after striking several matches to find the keyhole – he was able to unlock using a large old-fashioned iron key. Inside there was a cool domed chamber running back into the rock and, when he lit a candle and stuck it on one of the row of big wooden barrels lying on their sides, I finally realized where he had brought me. It was his *bodega* or wine cellar, where his own personal wine harvest was stored, and we were to sample last year's vintage to see how it was coming on. Not only were the previous years' produce stored there but, as he demonstrated at incomprehensible length, this was also where each year he made the wine himself. There were stone troughs and, I gathered, all sorts of complicated things which needed to be done to the grapes before their juice entered the barrels. We were there to taste the *clara*, which he extracted carefully from the first of the barrels into two dirty tumblers and held proudly up to the candlelight before urging me to taste it. It was a delicate very pale pink, which he told me would in time deepen to red. I had to admit it was delicious, which meant we had to try a lot more. '*Sin quím-icos*,' he exclaimed repeatedly as we smacked our lips.

We had seen doors set in the hillside before, without realizing what lay behind them. Now I saw that as well as finding a farmer inside every Spaniard one scratched, there would as likely as not be a winemaker as well.

'My family's vineyard is far away,' the old man told me, 'but I go and harvest the grapes and bring them to my own *bodega* every year.' From then on we were to recognize *bodegas* in quite surprising places in countryside and towns alike, and to appreciate how important it must be to have one's own wine as well as one's own vege-tables.

As we supported each other back into the village I reflected how my new friend was proudest of the fact that his wine contained no chemicals. Conventional wisdom would have us believe that country people long to escape the gruelling labour of their lives and swap the drudgery for cities where the streets are paved with gold. We are told that anyone who advocates the ideals of a rural life based on less consumption and less exploitative values is seeing the world through a Utopian vision of rose-covered cottages and a country life that never existed. Since the Industrial Revolution, it has been in the interests of those with products to manufacture and sell to mould the rest of the world to the idea that happiness can only be achieved through joining the market and abandoning self-supporting systems.

In fact, without rejecting modern technology and all the benefits that invention can bring, it is perfectly logical to wish to harness it to a less consumptive and less exploitative way of life, maintaining the integrity and standards of the past – wine without chemicals, for example – while reducing if not completely eliminating the hard work. After all, is not one of the major problems associated with modern life the lack of hard daily physical activity which, combined with a natural diet, keeps a body healthy? At least, that was the conclusion I came to as I rolled into town, almost as tired as I have ever been, and then walked the remaining 400 yards to the school carrying a heavy bale of alfalfa hay under each arm. Of course, there had been no question of being allowed to pay for anything.

DAY 11 Saturday 19th August   **TARDÁJOS TO HONTANAS**

Joan found a woman in the village who sold fresh milk from the cows occupying the ground floor of her house. She was asked if we were pilgrims and when she replied that we were, again payment was refused.

We all felt that we deserved a rest, at least until the cool of the evening; and so we left the horses in the playground, well supplied with hay, and drove back into Burgos.

One of the most important pilgrim hospitals on the Way lies on the outskirts of Burgos, the Hospital del Rey. As it was closed for major repairs, we could only see the outer courtyard with stone carvings and gargoyles on the wall, and the remarkable carved wooden doors of the chapel showing a series of vivid and rather moving scenes connected with the pilgrimage. Exhausted, near-naked pilgrims are shown toiling across stony country supporting each other and surrounded by saints and angels. It is an intimate glimpse into 16th-century life, the same gourd, leather scrip and wooden staff being carried as they were by much earlier travellers, but the clothes are rather more elaborate with woollen stockings and positively modern leather shoes. There was a child of Merlin's age being led by his father's hand, a suckling mother and a very limp-wristed St James leaning on his staff, who looked as though he could not kill a fly.

The mahogany from which the doors are carved may have been amongst the first to be brought from the New World, as they are part of the restorations carried out by the Hapsburg Emperor Charles V who ruled from 1516 to 1556, a period when the Americas were being opened up at an extraordinary pace. It was the first tangible link I saw in a chain of ideas linking the pilgrimage with the Conquest. Columbus received permission to go off on his second journey in Burgos, and much of the money for building, restoring or converting the huge churches along the Way to look as they do today came from the wealth of the New World.

Santiago Matamoros even appeared in South America leading the *conquistadores* in battles against the Indians, justifying the atrocities being carried out on them in the name of Christendom. There is a double irony in this, since it was just at this period that the pilgrimage began a gradual decline, until by the 18th and 19th centuries it was almost forgotten in the rest of Europe, where other revolutionary preoccupations were occupying the minds of the masses.

Close to the Hospital del Rey is the monastery of Las Huelgas, which was founded in 1187. Today the word is used for workers' strikes, but then it meant leisure and repose, because it was built originally as a pleasure ground and cool refuge from the heat of the Spanish plains. The King at that time was Alfonso VIII and he is buried there in a double sepulchre with his wife, Eleanor of England. She was a Plantagenet, one of the children of the English King Henry II and Eleanor of Aquitaine, born between Richard Coeur de Lion and John. It was at her request that Alfonso built the monastery, to which only ladies of the highest rank were admitted as Cistercian nuns and where they enjoyed extraordinary privileges, being exempt from taxes and so becoming extremely rich.

The pantheon in which their tomb lies, together with several others, is in the Nuns' Choir, under a soaring nave – a wonderful place to spend eternity with the one you love. Thick, polished floorboards were added in the 16th century, perhaps also from the Americas; there are 17th-century Beauvais tapestries from France on the walls and the tomb itself is simple, delicately carved and infinitely touching. Alfonso and Eleanor were married when he was fifteen (having already been king for twelve years) and she was only nine. The first of their two daughters was born when she was nineteen and after forty-four years of marriage they both died in the same year, 1214. It sounds like a love story and one would like to think that they had been allowed to rest in peace, but sadly their tomb and all but one of the others were desecrated by Napoleon's troops in 1809. The extra tragedy of this was that many of the court clothes, jewels and arms buried with the princes and princesses were stolen and are lost for ever. Those which survived are on show in the museum and they make one of the most fascinating collections I have seen anywhere. Gold and silver brocaded court costumes, which must have been dreadfully heavy and hot, reveal an intricacy and splendour in 12th- and 13th-century clothes which I had not suspected. There is a sophistication and a richness in the fabrics to match those of any court at any period of history anywhere in the world. I had always thought that the pre-Raphaelite image of the Middle Ages had been highly romanticized and exaggerated, yet here were Oriental, Moorish and Christian designs woven with consummate skill and artistry into the most splendid and opulent garments. And these were only the few that survived.

Next to the church are two cloisters, one 12th-century Romanesque and the other 13th-century Gothic, both ravishing examples of their respective styles of architecture and both with clear Moorish influences creeping into the designs. By now our eyes were becoming more accustomed to these peculiar mixtures. It was extremely interesting to find two such different cloisters right next to each other, and to have a chance to compare them directly and begin to try to understand their basic differences. It seemed to me that where Romanesque art is simple and sober, with barrel vaults and guileless, open sculptures, Gothic is all thrusting arches supported by flying buttresses, ornately decorated and with knowing sculptures of essentially worldly saints. We found ourselves being more and more drawn to the honesty of the Romanesque, an attitude which surprised me as until then I had always thought myself more attracted by the flamboyant and ornate end of the artistic spectrum. One should not generalize too sweepingly on these matters, but it did add greatly to the joy of travel through a region so supremely rich in medieval architecture to find ourselves developing quite strong likes and dislikes which we could share and exclaim about as new wonders continued to dazzle us.

Burgos Cathedral – to which we now returned – was, we decided, too large for our taste, too florid, too ornate, simply too much. We cut short our visit to go to a bar across the square and watch on television the Pope entering Santiago accompanied by tens of thousands of pilgrims as well as the King and Queen of Spain. The crowds surged and billowed in all directions; there was a manifest atmosphere of religious fervour; this was apparently how it must have been in the great days of the pilgrimage hundreds of years ago. And yet I could not help wondering as to the real motive of the largely young throng. Of course they were mostly good Christians and what they were doing was culturally correct, but did they believe that their sins mattered so much that they needed to travel to Santiago to have them expunged? Were they motivated by the same fear of hell and the same ecstasy at the prospect of heaven as their forebears, or did they have other preoccupations? There was no doubting their energy and enthusiasm, but were these now not largely far more temporal things than a perhaps selfish preoccupation with their own immortal souls? Wondering if all that vigour could not be more usefully directed towards issues which affected all life on earth rather than just our own, I rehearsed again my own heresy that man is not made in God's image. In any case, we were all extremely glad not to be in Santiago just then, but to have ahead of us the prospect of riding into our destination when things would be much more peaceful.

Being mobile on wheels for a few hours once more we drove south through theatrical escarpment country where barren rock-strewn hills, wild cliffs and eroded fields somehow nourished pretty villages, to Santo Domingo de Silos. There we hoped to see the cloisters which have been called the triumphant climax of Romanesque art in Spain, but the monastery was closed until 4.30 pm and nothing would persuade the monk who answered my ring to bend the rules. We dared not leave the horses unattended that long and so drove back by a different route, looking in on two small towns on the way. Covarrubias, to which we detoured simply because the country-side was so beautiful, astonished us by being a much restored village of quaint half-timbered houses, with gatehouse, massive walls and streets thronged with tourists. Every other shop was a restaurant or sold trinkets, and we might as well have been in Polperro or Capri. We had forgotten it was Saturday, but still it seemed extraordinary that so many people should have congregated somewhere so far off a main road. It was very pretty, but we did not linger. Much more to our taste was Lerma, which ironically does lie on a main road but seemed virtually deserted as we drove up on cobbled streets through the old part of the town to the great ducal square. Built by the rich and powerful Duke of Lerma in 1617, it is a rare example of classical town planning in Spain. The huge palace, noble apart-ments and public buildings also fell victim to the marauding French troops during the Peninsular War, and now it has the feel of a ghost town; but the stonework was mellow in the afternoon sun, the proportions distinguished, with a rare sense of space and light, and we liked it.

As we drove through Burgos on our way back to Tardájos, we passed our Belgian friend pushing his little cart and waved to him. Just beyond we spotted a hitch-hiker beside the road with a card-board sign on which was written 'León', and recognized the young Frenchman with whom we had talked the day before as he walked alongside the girl from Quimper. Not a proper pilgrim after all, he did nothing to restore our opinion of the descendants of Napoleon's vandalous troops, and feeling virtuous and British we returned to our horses.

By 5.15 we were in the saddle again and heading across empty open farmland into a stiff head-wind, which kept us all pleasantly cool. At first there were expanses of gold stubble where we went fast, then a higher plateau with stone in heaps and built into walls. It reminded me of Connemara. The villages we passed through were friendly and the track between them well marked but free of any other traffic. In the first village, Rabe de las Calzadas, we were chased by a young Alsatian bitch which snapped at our heels and barked. Instead of heading back as we rode out into the fields, she stayed with us, racing off to chase birds and returning panting and wagging her tail. In spite of our efforts to discourage her and send her home, she seemed to decide to adopt us and to be making overtures to us demonstrating what a good dog she was. Agreeable though it would be to have a dog with us each day, the chances of her surviving the next main road we met were small, and we discussed how we could persuade her to leave us. An amiable farmer walking home from one empty horizon to another, a wooden hay-rake over his shoulder, stopped for a chat. Once we had settled the question of our destination and he had confirmed that his crops had done well, we asked him if he would like to relieve us of our new companion, but he declined with a laugh saying that he had enough dogs already, although he conceded that she was a nice looker. We need not have worried, as it turned out. Passing the first houses of Hontanas we were set on by a pack of barking curs, who soon transferred their attentions from our horses to our dog and drove her yelping back the way we had come.

Our ground crew was full of beans, having received an especially friendly welcome in what the *Guide to Spain*, produced by the Confraternity of St James in London, describes as 'possibly the best pilgrim village of all'. We were all to sleep in a well-equipped refuge above the bar, where there was a dormitory of bunk beds, and the horses could graze in a safe enclosure below our window. Joan had already started cooking supper outside and we were soon tucking in to lamb chops and tomatoes.

After this we were joined by a priest from Madrid, who published children's books and was full of information about the area. He told us that Hontanas came from the Latin Fontanas, because the hills around were bursting with springs. It seemed a potentially prosperous little place and we heard that there were plans to encourage pilgrims to stop there more often and enjoy the amenities. A small swimming-pool had recently been completed . . .

We were not the only pilgrims in Hontanas that night. A charming middle-aged French couple who had walked from Paris joined us in the bar later as we wrote up our journals. It was hard to talk much as the bar filled up with twenty of the noisiest of the villagers who played cards, ignored the television, drank and shouted cheerfully at each other. There was a feeling of contentment and harmony which is only found in close communities where everyone is known to everyone else and travellers, while welcome, are politely excluded. As on many other evenings during this journey, it was brought home to us that there is no comparison between the quality of rural serenity and the harsh edge of urban life where every face in the street is that of a stranger.

DAY 12 Sunday 20th August　　　　　HONTANAS TO FRÓMISTA

D awn is the time to see wildlife. Once the sun is high in the sky, it becomes dangerous to be out in the open where sharp watching eyes rise high above the ground on thermals and men are out in the fields with guns and pointers. Hares loped languidly out of our way, pausing to sit up and look back at us, almost as though inviting a chase. Medieval travellers used to fear them as witches, but pilgrims were protected by the sanctity of their journey. A pair of bee-eaters cavorted together like colourful harlequins and the partridges and quail were out in force, whirring to right and left as the clatter of our hooves disturbed them and the stillness of the morning.

We reached the vestiges of the hospital of San Anton while the sun was still low enough in the sky to shine through the delicate silhouettes of the remaining arches and windows, making the ruins seem ephemeral and fragile. They were built in the 14th century on 12th-century foundations by French friars, followers of the first Christian monk, St Anthony of Egypt – not to be confused with the much later St Anthony of Padua, patron of the poor and finder of lost property. This was the 4th-century hermit who wrestled with the devil and was afflicted with all manner of unpleasant temptations and pestilences. His intercession was sought by those who suffered from erysipelas, known as the sacred fire, St Anthony's fire, or 'the rose', a contagious inflammation of the skin producing large blisters which during its height in the 11th century often proved fatal. He was also the patron saint of swineherds, which is interesting because the disease with which he was associated is today rare in men, but still common as swine erysipelas, a serious threat to pigs.

Many miraculous cures were attributed to his curative powers and sick people flocked to be ministered to by the monks, who used to lead them through the countryside playing on flutes like pied pipers: probably as good a health cure as any other. Our priest of the night before told us another version of the legend, designed to boost Spanish pride. Many of the pilgrims, he said, came from far away across Europe and hoped, on their way to Santiago, to seek treatment from St Anthony for bad digestions and upset stomachs. At home they ate lousy bread and drank filthy wine, so it was hardly surprising that they should suffer as they did. By the time they had crossed the Pyrenees and begun to eat good Spanish food they were already on the way to recovery and so the Saint's reputation as a healer was proved again and again.

In the wall of the grand archway through which the pilgrims had to pass were two deep alcoves. Those who had mistimed their journey and arrived to find the great gates locked, so that they must walk on through the night, would discover loaves of bread left out there for them by the kindly friars. Now they and the monastery itself are empty and crumbling. Shards of broken glass line the walls to stop enthusiasts climbing them and hastening the decay, but wind and rain and time are doing the job anyway.

Ahead of us now lay the ancient Roman town of Castrojeriz, in a picturesque setting at the foot of a round terraced hill crowned by a ruined 13th-century castle. As we rode through the sleepy streets which girdled the slopes, we passed three handsome old churches, but all were closed and so we saw only their seasoned exteriors. The saffron stone of which they were built made them seem a part of the very earth on which they had stood for a thousand years. On a wall beside the pilgrim route were carved two realistic skulls and crossbones, emblems of mortality. A warning, we thought, that the Way ahead was about to become harder, but actually they are probably an indication that the Knights Templar once had a house there, since this was their symbol long before it appeared on pirate flags and electricity pylons. Relaxing on a bench in the sun we saw the girl from Quimper, happy with her day of rest in such tranquil surroundings. We expected to meet again and again over the coming weeks, but she never caught us up and that was the last we saw of her.

Now we had a steep ridge to cross on foot, leading the horses on an uneven trail, hot and barren but made delightful by the increasingly breathtaking view back across the plain we had just crossed. In addition, we seemed to be on a glass mountain. At first we actually thought, with disgust, that the remains of broken bottles littered the path. Then, when we looked closer, we found that many of the stones beneath our feet were crystals which glinted in the sun. We gathered up a few to take home, where they were identified as gypsum. The momentary glister must have cheered many weary pilgrims as they toiled over this obstacle down the centuries. As we left one plain behind, walked briskly across a level plateau – too short to warrant mounting – and were then greeted by another sweep of open yellow landscape reaching to the far horizon, I felt as close to all those who had gone before us as at any moment on our pilgrimage. Although there was not a single human figure to be made out behind or ahead of us, and the Way meandered in each direction as far as our eyes could see, every previous foot must have trod where we were treading and for a moment it seemed that an unnumbered host walked with us. Strangely, it was a comforting rather than a frightening thought.

Flaming, thirsty hours through a parched countryside followed, where the secret was not to think of water since we carried none with us. Then, unexpectedly the Fuente del Piojo (the Fountain of the Louse), where ice-cold, fresh water poured straight out of a hillside into a clean cattle trough, so that we and the horses could enjoy the relief to the full together. Our pleasure would have been only a fraction as great had we been taking sips along the way and had our mouths not been dry and our lips beginning to crack. How our medieval predecessors must have revelled at this spot, stripped off their rags and washed from their malodorous bodies the lice which gave the place its name.

We were now deep in the heartland of the once rival petty king-doms which caused so many castles to be built and gave Castile its name. These endless high plains, the Meseta, were where the mercen-ary armies of Christian warlords fought their usually inconclusive battles or united from time to time to take on the Moors and dream of the Reconquest which took so very long to achieve, even with Saint James's help. It was also the country of El Cid, the greatest legendary hero of Spain, who died in 1099. Glorified in Spain's best known epic poem and portrayed heroically by Charlton Heston in the film of the same name, his story seems more like a fable than fact; but he was real enough, and recent scholarship has shown how mercenary and bloodthirsty warfare was in those days. The passionate religious idealism and the striving after spiritual and architectural beauty contrast strangely with the brutality and greed of those who directed the course of history.

The Río Pisuerga used at one time to mark the border between Castile and León, whose name has nothing to do with lions but is derived from the presence of the Roman Seventh Legion, whose garrison in the 1st century A.D. was the foundation of the present city. The river is spanned by a 12th-century bridge of eleven arches, unexpected both in its elegance and in the sudden lushness around it. Deep green grass, rushes and limpid pools are shaded by whispering poplars. It was the perfect spot for a picnic and our French friends of the night before, having started very early in the morning and not dawdled on the way, were stretched out in the shade of the parapet. Their name was Petraud and they later wrote to us to say that they had followed the traces of our 'magnifiques montures' until they finally disappeared on the granite of Galicia. They themselves were to reach Santiago on the 9th September after walking 1,750 kilometres. '*Quel merveilleux périple*,' they exclaimed joyfully.

Having nothing with us to eat, we rode on into Itero de la Vega, a most friendly place where in the village shop we bought two giant slices of water melon, two pears, two pastry cakes, and two ice-creams which we ate right away. The rest we carried a couple of miles beyond the town to a single tree in the open plain, where we unsaddled and, letting the horses graze, rested for an hour. Through half-closed eyes I watched the distant figure of a shepherd beneath a black umbrella gradually creep nearer until he could inspect us at close quarters. But he was too shy to come and talk, pretending he had business elsewhere when I called out a greeting to him, and simply raising a hand as he, his dogs and his flock continued their crablike progress over the ground.

For a time in the afternoon we rode beside a wide canal, and crowded reed-beds gave shelter to all kinds of furtive unseen wildlife. Fish, frogs and terrapins plopped as we passed; small birds and perhaps river-bank mammals like water-rats and moles messed about, rustling and fluttering under the wind in the willows. It was a more intimate and less exhausting world than the desiccated plains on either side.

Frómista was once a major halt on the pilgrim route; now it is a sleepy little place with a population of little over a thousand. In the tranquil central square is one of the most perfect Romanesque churches in Europe, all that remains of a once great monastery dedicated to the French St Martin, patron saint of innkeepers and drunkards. Purists complain that it was over-restored a century ago, but we were unaware of this as we gasped at its sheer presence. Like a handful of other great buildings around the world – the Acropolis, Machu Picchu, Ankor Wat – it is absolutely right, growing out of the ground as though from deep tap-roots, perfectly situated in time and space. The lines of the walls and roofs, the curves of towers and apse blend with a flawless poetry which imprinted the idea of Romanesque on us, so that we looked at each other and said aloud, 'So that's what it's all about.' Although all trace of the monastic buildings is supposed to have vanished, on our horses we were able to see over a high wall nearby into a wild secret garden, where pigeons fluttered around an ancient crumbling dovecote.

In 1190, a century and a half after the monastery and church were founded in Frómista, one Pedro Gonzalez Telmo was born there. He was to become a Dominican friar, devote his life to the poor fishermen of Galicia and in time to become the patron saint of sailors. As St Elmo he is remembered wherever his 'fire', also called the corposant, plays round the masts of ships during a storm. I saw it once on a tramp ship in the North Pacific; the electric discharge which causes the fire made my own hair stand on end and gave me a nasty fright.

An hour out of town we found that our faithful ground crew had set up camp beside the small hermitage of San Miguel in a grove of poplars, where there was lush grass and a fountain where we could wash the day's dust off ourselves and our mounts. Merlin had had a good day at a municipal swimming-pool, where he had been made much of by mothers and children alike. With less than 30 miles a day to drive, he and Joan were beginning to enjoy themselves and feel less burdened by the responsibility of finding somewhere for us all to sleep each night.

The moon was huge and orange behind the simple building with its little bell tower, the night breeze was balmy and life was good.

DAY 13 Monday 21st August   **FRÓMISTA TO MORATINOS**

There is something very restful and fulfilling about closing one's eyes on a rising moon and opening them to see the sun becoming visible over the same horizon.

My only constant worry was the place on Duque's back, which I was convinced was going to turn into a sore. Each night I sluiced it with cold water, then poured on raw alcohol when it was dry; and each morning it had miraculously grown new skin and hair to look almost as good as new. Now, as I picked out his feet I saw that another problem was developing. One of his shoes was loose, and most of his and Guadalquivir's were wafer-thin. We would have to find a blacksmith soon. I had brought some nails from Pablo's stable in Estella and was able to fix the loose one fairly satisfactorily, but we had no spare shoes and in any case I do not trust myself to shoe two horses from scratch without laming one of them.

Pleasant riding along a now tree-lined canal with a level earth tow-path helped us to make good time in the morning. There were golden orioles in the poplars and the water was clear for once: we even passed a fisherman. Another hermitage, the Virgen de Río, greeted us as we turned on to a gravel road; it consisted of a solid church with a pleasant colonnaded rectory built on to the side. It seemed to us that the hermits living along the Way had rather comfortable lives.

An old man with a single tooth in the centre of his top gum stopped us and asked if we were pilgrims. According to our map some miles of roadwork lay ahead, but he pointed out to us a cross-country route which led us straight to Carrión de los Condes. Twice the size of Frómista and an important town dominating the flat surrounding country, tall corn silos rose up on the outskirts. But we knew one of the hardest and most desolate stretches of our journey lay just beyond, and we felt we must not set out without at least trying to have the horses' feet seen to. We rode straight to the Guardia Civil barracks and I showed the cheerful sergeant there our letter from his General Jefe saying that we would be given every assistance. 'For the first time since leaving Roncesvalles,' I told him, 'we have a problem. We need a blacksmith.' 'No problem,' he replied. 'What's your second problem?' When I explained that every-thing else was well under control and we would not trouble them further, I thought all would be resolved quickly, and for a time there was a certain amount of bustle, with minions being sent to search for José, El Barbas, the bearded one, who had a reputation as a blacksmith but who could not be found. The trouble was that we had picked the very worst day of the year to need him, as it was the day of the Fiesta of Santa María del Camino, patron of the town, and El Barbas was a singer in one of the groups currently celebrating the event in the church.

It was two hours before they came out and the moment was worth waiting for, although we did not think so as we held the horses in the street and fretted about how far we still had to go that day. Suddenly the doors of the great south portal burst open. Beneath the arch of carved figures showing the Elders of the Apocalypse appeared the Virgin herself, borne on the shoulders of twelve young men in bright tee-shirts. A stiff, lifeless, modern wooden figure in a toga, she and her litter were bounced high into the air every few yards, the plastic flowers with which she was surrounded flopping their petals and artificial foliage. Crowds of young people filled the street and ran along beside, many in group uniforms such as striped monks' habits or straw hats. Grotesque masks hung on the walls of the houses by which she passed, music came in a cacophony from several bands, voices were raised in laughter and cheering; clearly there was much afoot and much to come. We would have liked to linger and join in the festivities, but we had a rendezvous before nightfall and many miles to go and so we searched for a bearded figure. Failing to spot him, I was at last directed to a bar where I found him serving himself and others behind the counter. Although fairly drunk already, he greeted me cheerfully and went to fetch his gear from the boot of his car. Using our nails, as he had neither these nor spare shoes, he efficiently removed those shoes that were loose, filed down the hooves and replaced them firmly. Accepting a generous donation for his trouble, he left us to our fate.

It was now early afternoon, one of the hottest days of the year, and soon we were alone in an endless stony waste. There was nothing to be seen in all directions except the track which stretched ahead of us die-straight to the horizon. It reminded us strongly of the Gobi desert and we suffered from heat, boredom and hard, sweaty saddles in equal parts. The sky was utterly cloudless and the monotony of the landscape infinitely depressing. I thought back to our ride across China. My most distinct memory was of the daunting distances, the barren northern wastelands apparently squeezed dry of all goodness by man's continuous over-use. Equally disheartening was the pity I felt for a people who, through the horrors of the Cultural Revolution, seemed paradoxically to have lost their culture entirely. It was quite a different pity from that I feel for those who are starving, refugees or oppressed, but closer to that prompted by the newly urbanized immigrants of Third World countries who find themselves in shanty-towns around the fringes of big cities. To lose one's identity is the greatest loss, worse than hunger or pain, for those may end – but how do you find yourself again if the tenets of your faith, culture, belief in how life works, in divine laws and taboos are taken from you? No one can sustain enthusiasm for new ideologies for very long, and when disillusionment sets in the support of a sure and ancient certainty may have gone. Christianity took on the holy places and many of the practices and ceremonies of the old religions it supplanted. What appeals to me most about the new green philosophies which are emerging is that they, too, return to natural and primal roots.

Towards evening we saw buildings and a church tower far ahead, and began to imagine a bar with cold drinks, or perhaps ice-creams. Like so many before us, we imagined that our small ordeal was over. For some miles we had been leading the horses on foot to spare them and so we walked into Calzadilla de la Cueza just as pilgrims have been doing for a thousand years. Three old ladies in black sat outside a doorway and watched us approach; there was something sinister and gleeful about the way they seemed to be measuring us. 'Is there water for the horses?' I asked. 'No,' they replied cheerfully. 'How about a bar for us then?' '*Tampoco*,' came the answer and now the glee was unmistakable. Literally meaning 'As little', I have always found this colloquial way of saying 'We don't have that either' rather irritating, but never more so than then. However, I managed a cheerful grin and said as convincingly as I could, 'Oh well, it doesn't matter. We're none of us very thirsty anyway.' Their disappointment at our stiff upper lips was palpable and it was clear that we were failing to respond as expected – and hoped. There was water rationing, they explained, and none would be forthcoming for some hours.

Just as we were preparing to mount up and ride to the next village, a bent old lady with Parkinson's disease came out of her house and, seeing our plight, immediately invited us into her courtyard. There she not only filled buckets for the horses from her own supply, but produced a bottle of iced water from her refrigerator and pressed us to drink our fill. True Christian charity, which we all accepted gratefully.

Two more grinding hours, now beside a busy country road, brought us to Moratinos, where we found another good camp in a grove of trees. Two leaping figures welcomed us, the smaller racing up to be hauled on to his mother's saddle so that he could ride the last few hundred yards in triumph. More Christian charity greeted us in the village where we went in search of feed for Duque and Guadalquivir. In a barn where several men were bagging and sifting great heaps of grain from the recent harvest, our needs were discussed at some length and a judicious mixture of last year's oats and barley was blended, shovelled into a large fibre sack and presented to us. I explained that I was a farmer myself, knew the value of grain and insisted on paying what was fair; but all to no avail.

The gentle breeze soughing in the poplars sounded like heavy rain and gale-force winds; the headlights of occasional passing lorries swept over our camp; the horses were restless and we slept fitfully, worrying about our simple equestrian problems but revelling in being horizontal for a while.

LEÓN

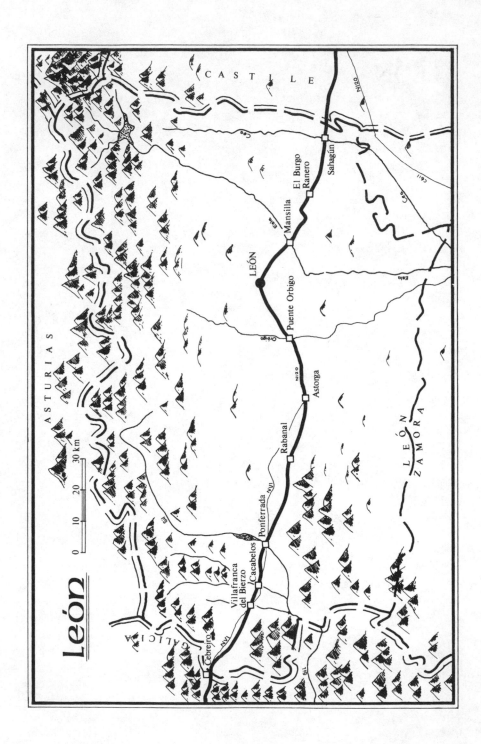

León

CASTILE

ASTURIAS

GALICIA

LEÓN ZAMORA

Sahagún
El Burgo Ranero
Mansilla
LEÓN
Puente Orbigo
Astorga
Rabanal
Ponferrada
Cacabelos
Villafranca del Bierzo
Cebreiro

30 km
20
10
0

Our chief problem was of course the horses' shoes, which would not last another day. Desperate measures were again called for, since none of our helpful village friends knew of a blacksmith anywhere in the vicinity.

Sahagún was only an hour away and we rode through the centre of the busy market town asking the way to the Guardia Civil. This time we were received by a captain, no less, who knew all about us, having read the circular letter and our itinerary. Our horses were allowed into the inner yard of the barracks, where the garages turned out to have been stables in the recent past and still had hay-racks and rings on the walls. A serious search was then made for a blacksmith. The best bet turned out to have died recently but soon there was rapid talk of another, although my Spanish was not immediately up to the subleties of why he was second best. It was explained more slowly to me that there were three problems. First he was almost blind; second he had no shoes, nor could he make any; and third he could not be found, being rumoured to be out shooting. The captain assured me that search parties had been despatched, but that we would have to track down some shoes ourselves. 'The army in León have a cavalry unit. I will ring my friend Commandante Cristobal at their HQ and see if he can help,' he said. After some cheerful banter and a glowing description of us and our horses, the instrument was passed to me: the Commandante wished to speak to me directly. 'What are your horses like?' he enquired. 'Well, they are about 15 hands, with small feet,' I replied. 'They are not exactly noble Andalusians of the finest quality.' He chuckled and said he understood exactly what I meant. Three complete sets of shoes of various sizes would be despatched by Guardia vehicle at once, and should be with us in an hour or so. This should satisfy our immediate needs but in two days, when we reached León, his own master farrier would do the whole job again properly. Unfortunately he could not offer to accommodate our horses at his barracks, since they had some quality stallions there and while the African Horse Sickness scare lasted no other horses were allowed, but he was sure the Guardia Civil would look after us. It was all too good to be true.

The captain suggested that we now relax for a while until action was again required. Louella and Joan decided they had some shopping to do and went into the centre of town with Merlin. I was invited to have a drink. The captain's chauffeur held open the door of the official car for me, while the sergeant and his boss got into the back. I removed my travel-stained leather chaps and hung them on a peg in the guardroom, then we drove up a couple of narrow cobbled streets and pulled up by a café. Up the stairs was a chic bar with white-painted tables and cane chairs, a terrace with umbrellas and a fine view, as well as every conceivable drink. It was like being transported into the Marbella Club and quite unexpected in a town of 2,700 inhabitants which does not even rate an entry in the Michelin *Green Guide*. In Ian Robertson's *Blue Guide*, Sahagún is described as 'a decaying and crumbling town. . . . the starting point late in December 1809 of the retreat of Sir John Moore's army to La Coruña'.

The captain came from Ceuta, the Spanish enclave in Morocco on the coast of Africa. We discovered that we had both travelled with the Tuareg in the Sahara and shared an admiration for their fortitude and self-reliance. The drinks – for which to my increasing shame I was never allowed to pay – flowed and the time passed animatedly as the sergeant and chauffeur contributed their view that civilization ended at the Straits of Gibraltar, called by them 'el Estrecho'.

Back at the barracks some time later, we found that neither blacksmith nor shoes had yet arrived. A young man from the mayor's office was waiting for the captain's permission to climb the ruined tower (which could only be reached through the barracks) and wind the clock. He asked if I would like to go with him and, since I would have a good view out over the town, I agreed. The wooden steps and later ladder up the tower were heart-stoppingly rickety, only loosely attached to the crumbling stonework and supported here and there by rotting beams. Half-way up, as several pigeons burst out of a cavity and nearly knocked me off my perch, I began to regret my decision, but there were some traces of Romanesque windows to take my mind off things and the clock mechanism was a wonder of Heath Robinson ingenuity. Winding it required substantial strength, using levers and cogs, and while he bent himself to the task the young man revealed a wide interest in the history of the region.

In the winter of 1808 Sir John Moore, 'the greatest trainer of troops the British army has ever known',* was in charge of the small British force helping the Spanish guerilla army to fight the French, Napoleon having placed his brother Joseph on the Spanish throne. Moore, believing his allies to be defeated, wanted to withdraw to Portugal but was persuaded by the Spanish who were desperately holding on to Madrid to try to attack the French forces of Marshal Soult on the Carrión River, so as to create a diversion. At first the

* *Encyclopaedia Britannica.*

campaign went well and outside Sahagún a great cavalry battle was fought at daybreak on the 21st December. The 15th (The King's) Hussars, after riding all night in freezing conditions with between 300 and 400 men and horses, routed about 800 French Dragoons and Chasseurs. Twenty Frenchmen were killed, 167 prisoners taken, including 2 lieutenant-colonels, at a cost of only 4 men and 4 horses lost to the Hussars. In commemoration of this action the 15th Hussars were awarded the 'Battle Honour' of Sahagún, which they were thereafter entitled to carry on their standard.

For the next two days they chased the retreating French and advanced towards Soult, preparing to attack him at Carrión de los Condes. Then everything suddenly changed. Word reached Sir John Moore that the Emperor, hearing about what was happening, had diverted troops which were marching towards Portugal and was himself leading another 50,000 men at full speed to cut off the English army. With a peculiar echo of Roland's recognition at Roncesvalles that this number of reinforcements spelt doom, Moore ordered his troops to retreat. By an even stranger coincidence many of the survivors of what followed were themselves to fight at Roncesvalles five years later when the French were finally thrown out of Spain by Wellington.

Then began one of the most terrible retreats in British military history as Moore and his men were harried by the French over 250 miles of wild snowbound country dying of frostbite, hunger and their wounds. The horses fared even worse. By now they were 'completely worn out; many of them . . . so crippled as to make it absolutely necessary to destroy them, so that every ten yards you met with a dead or dying horse, and in many places ten, fifteen or twenty together'. This description was written by a Colonel Vivian, who was later to acquit himself with distinction at the Battle of Waterloo (where he captured Napoleon's baggage train), and to receive a title and an estate in Cornwall – of which, by another odd quirk, some of my farm was once a part. It took them three weeks to reach Corunna where, in the final battle as they were being evacuated by the British Navy, Sir John Moore died of his wounds while holding off the French. His tomb is lovingly preserved in the San Carlos Garden, shaded by tall English elms. Carved in large stone letters nearby are the words of the poem by which he is best remembered: 'Not a drum was heard, not a funeral note . . .'

Long before these events Sahagún was a very important place. The crumbling tower on which we stood was almost all that remains of what was once the greatest monastery in Spain, with beds for sixty pilgrims and with fifty priories and abbeys dependent on it. According to dubious legend the church was founded by Charlemagne, and it may well have been the westernmost point he reached in his campaigns, but a date of 904 – nearly 100 years after his death – is more usually given for the establishment of the monastery.

In the 16th century Sahagún produced two great men, both friars, who in quite different ways pioneered new subjects. Fray Pedro Ponce de León, member of a great family from León which included Juan, the discoverer of Florida, was the first man to teach the deaf to speak, read and write. Before his time it had been believed that they were incapable of education, and his methods formed the basis of subsequent systems. At just the same time as Brother Pedro was struggling with his afflicted pupils in Sahagún itself, another alumnus of the monastery, Fray Bernardo de Sahagún, was in the New World watching the devastating effects of colonization on the Aztecs in Mexico. In a monumental work called *A General History of the Things of New Spain*, he recorded in Aztec, Spanish and Latin all that he could about pre-Columbian civilization, with illustrations of the flora and fauna. He was one of the first Europeans to describe rubber. Even more significant was the information he gleaned from the Indians, whom he troubled to question about their world and their gods at a time when most of his contemporaries still regarded them as animals without souls who could be slaughtered freely and who knew nothing. He has been called the founder of modern ethnology.

I like to think that as young boys Pedro and Bernardo may have sat beside each other in class while some wise monk inspired them both to go out and change the world for the better.

From the tower there was a fine view out over the red pantile roofs and thick walls of Sahagún. To the west, where we were headed, the land was flat and featureless to the horizon and I felt a sudden strong desire to get this dry part of our journey over with and reach green fields and hills again. Far below us in the Guardia Civil courtyard there was activity and we saw that both the vehicle from León – with the post-haste shoes – and the blacksmith had arrived.

He really was almost blind with the thickest of pebble glasses, and I had to guide his hammer hand as he banged in the nails. Nevertheless his touch was sure and he did a good job, so that we felt there was a fair chance of our reaching León without more trouble. Mid-afternoon and still some 35 kilometres to go by night-fall as we rode out of town. Another endless stony plain with a rough farm track running across it and little to relieve the monotony or take our minds off the discomfort . . . except that Duque lost a hind shoe almost immediately. Luckily I heard the tinkle as it fell and so was able to nail it on again; but for the rest of that day we worried about losing more. His other hind shoe had split and clinked with each step, which did nothing for our nerves.

Ann Askew's martyrdom as shown in the Hanbury family pedigree
(after the illustration in Foxe's *Book of Martyrs*)

Louella praying inside the Chapel at Eunate

Louella riding
Guadalquivir for
the first time beside
the stream at
Roncesvalles.

Below: Cooling off
in the river at
Larasoaña after the
first day of riding.

Top: A hill village rising out of the morning mist on the plain near Pamplona.

Above: The note left under a stone on a waymark, with two imperial mints for those following on foot.

Merlin on the little white
stallion which later bit
him.

Below: Louella and Robin
outside the Monastery of
Irache.

Top: A graveyard of old milestones at Los Arcos.

Above: The Tapestry of Santiago Matamoros in the Parador at Santo Domingo de la Calzada

Merlin and Louella giving Guadalquivir a drink at Villafranca Montes de Oca.

Below: Camping on the church steps at Villafranca Montes de Oca.

Louella's hair was the same colour as the fresh straw on the stubble fields.

Below: For much of Way we walked, leading the horses over stony ground or on steep stretches.

The Bishop's Palace at Astorga, built by the Art Nouveau architect Antonio Gaudi.

Below: A shepherd with his dogs and his flock near Itero de la Vega.

Top: Below the romantic walls of the Templar castle at Ponferrada.

Above: The rose window in Leon Cathedral, the colours as rich as ever after letting the sunshine through for 700 years.

Duque and Guadalquivir look back from
the glass mountain over the plain we had
just crossed.

Top: Venerable Spanish chestnuts gave us welcome shade as we neared Cebreiro.

Above: A Galician farmer driving his cows home to milk in the evening.

The main altar at Vilar de Doñas with the
astonishing 14th-century painting of Christ. Both
were damp and covered with green mould.
Below: The figure of San Roque in Padron Church.

Above: In the same church there is a marvellous
St James on his white horse slaughtering Moors.

'I have seen dawn and sunset on moors and windy hills
Coming in solemn beauty like slow old tunes of Spain'

Top: Castro de Barona, the old Celtic settlement on a headland on the Atlantic coast.

Above: The big bales of modern farming give a surreal feel to the ancient Spanish plains.

Half-way, the strangely named village of El Burgo Ranero loomed above the horizon and sank beneath it once more behind us. It seemed to have nothing to recommend it except a good fountain for the horses. On for hour after hour past occasional welcome gullies where we would say what good camp-sites they would have made if we had only known to rendezvous there. Everywhere was covered with loose stones, so that we could seldom canter to relieve the tedium. Worst of all was the litter which appeared whenever we neared 'civilization'. Each village seemed to have a shallow scrape in the ground about a kilometre outside it, to which the people toiled with their rubbish. Once upon a time there was probably just an unpleasant smell of biodegrading matter for the traveller to endure as he passed these places. Today the litter is carried in black plastic bin-liners, filled with other plastic bags which blow in the wind to scatter their contents far and wide. The landscape fluttered and glinted in the sunlight as wind and sun caught the detritus of our society – tins, aluminium foil, foam rubber, expanded polystyrene, rubbish which would not disappear but would, we felt, continue to grow and spread until the whole of Spain was covered by it. No effort seemed to be being made to confine, bury or burn it, and for us it was the most depressing aspect of Spain. Often we would find unspeakable packages from which disposable nappies, old under-wear and worn-out sneakers spilled, carefully deposited behind the trees to which we planned to tie our horses for the night. Rivers were especially tempting foci for dumping litter, and we regularly saw people gleefully tipping their waste over bridges. Perhaps their entry into the Common Market may open the Spaniards' eyes to this least excusable form of pollution, although the problem is just as bad in other countries around the Mediterranean.

The best change would be not to try to impose more technological solutions to a problem created by technology, but to change the hearts and minds of the people themselves. Instead of bigger bull-dozers for burying the stuff deeper and fibreglass septic tanks which need emptying, a belief in conservation, beauty, a clean environment and a healthy world for all life would be a much better answer. In a country where the rural population is being catapulted into a consumer economy from a relatively sustainable if grindingly hard medieval one, the only way of bringing about this change is through a force as powerful as the church. Green philosophy may have that strength, and there is certainly nothing in it incompatible with the basic tenets of conventional religions. The introspective and essen-tially selfish search for personal salvation, which drove so many millions to go on pilgrimages, could become a noble communal effort to save the world from man's self-destructive greed, which can so easily lead to the destruction of all life.

Reeling from exhaustion we reached Mansilla de las Mulas, our destination, as darkness fell at 9.00 pm, to find that the unpleasant man in charge of the refuge had misinformed Joan – or perhaps failed to believe in our existence – and that there was after all nowhere there for the horses to spend the night. Wearily – but anxiously, as setting up camp after dark would be difficult – we crossed to the far bank of the Río Esla where there was a grove of poplars where some people were already camped. They proved to be gypsies, and on the advice of the helpful citizenry who had followed us out of town we pitched our tents as far away from them as possible. '*Gitanos*,' 'bad people,' they said. 'They will steal your horses and everything else in the night'. Deep in our luggage I had packed a swordstick against just such an occurrence, and now I dug it out and put it under my pillow.

There was a café nearby where we went for something to eat, taking it in turns so that our camp would not be left unattended. An old black and white Errol Flynn 'B' movie was playing on the television, and we watched him clear a ship's deck of pirates with his fine swordsmanship as we munched our bread and meat. My first wife, Marika, and I spent several days with him once in Havana, just after the Cuban revolution. The only prominent Westerner to identify with Castro's guerrillas, he was a great hero with the wild young boys and girls who had occupied the town. Once, as we were returning to our hotel in the small hours after a night out at the legendary Tropicana night-club (which still functioned in spite of the war and the absence of any tourists), Errol spotted a milk float on which wooden barrels of milk were drawn by six white mules. For him it was an irresistible prop from one of his films, and he thrust a bundle of notes into the muleteer's hand so that we might take over. Then, cracking the whip above the startled animals' heads he drove them wildly through the deserted streets. Milk slopped out of the barrels to which we clung for our lives, while the revolutionary troops on patrol shouted '*Olé, El Flynn*' and urged us on.

I was quietly remembering all that and fantasizing about taking on the gypsies with my swordstick when Joan in her white nightie came running in saying that there were drunken men shouting all round the tents. 'I had to leave Merlin there, asleep,' she gasped. Together we flew back through the trees, leaving Louella to settle up and follow. It was by now pitch-dark and in the torchlight the scene was unreal, but frightening: flickering shadows and the pale shapes of our grazing animals as we drew near. But all was well. The noise had come from an innocent group of revellers now disappearing in the distance, having passed along a path which Joan had been unaware went close to our camp. There was no sign of life from the gypsies, but we still slept lightly that night.

DAY 15 Wednesday 23rd August
                    MANSILLA DE LAS MULAS TO LEÓN

Our first sight of the *gitanos* revealed them sitting on the steps of their caravan in the misty dawn; the girl in flared red skirt and with a bright shawl around her shoulders leisurely peeled potatoes; the young man lay back, his long legs in black trousers slightly higher than his head, taking his ease. We scurried about, eager to be under way before traffic built up on the road we would have to follow for much of the way into León. They never turned their heads to look at us, as though they knew what we had been thinking about them.

The army's master farrier was called Jesus Olmo and he looked the part to a T, burly and black-bearded. He and his team of three apprentices were waiting for us at the León Guardia Civil HQ and, under his instruction, they set to work. Each hoof was pared down, each shoe was hammered into shape on an anvil. Much time was spent eyeing up the fit and making slight adjustments before each nail was located and relocated until the master was satisfied. Once each foot was completed the horse was led up and down while its gait was critically examined to see if everything was comfortable. This, we could see, was an operation which was going to take some time and the horses would never be in better hands.

We drove off to find somewhere to stay for the couple of nights we planned to be in León. Five kilometres out of town at La Virgen del Camino there was a large Dominican seminary which we knew welcomed pilgrims. A splendid old white-robed and bearded father greeted us and said that, while they had never accommodated horses before, he saw no reason why they should not be able to do so. A young friar called Xavier, who was stripped to the waist and building a brick wall, took us to an unoccupied courtyard. Dried-up weeds, which would give the horses something to chew on, grew on the baked ground and a bare room with mattresses on the floor and very basic sanitation would do nicely for us. We thanked him and said we would ride out later.

Back in the barracks we found that Joan and Merlin had become the centre of attention for most of the children in the cantonment. Merlin was being swung enthusiastically on one thing after another in the playground, while Joan had half a dozen pretty young girls holding her hands and chattering away in incomprehensible Spanish. The blacksmiths were just finishing oiling the hooves of our rather stunned horses, who had never received treatment quite like this before and almost certainly never would again. Then they left, refusing payment or reward of any sort, Jesus stating formally that he did not expect us to have any problems, but should anything occur during the next few days, while we were still in reach of León, he would drive out himself and put it right.

I was summoned to the offices of the Guardia Civil Lieutenant, an elegant, languid gentleman of the old school who assured me that we had only to ask and anything would be provided. Sadly, due to the African Horse Sickness, accommodation at the army stables was as we knew impossible; but he had taken it on himself to arrange for our horses to be looked after at the Club Hippique, which happened to be just across the street. This was an offer it was impossible to refuse. We rode there, Duque and Guadalquivir stepping gingerly but soundly on their new shoes, and found rows of huge, wild-looking stallions in stalls, who neighed noisily as our suddenly unimpressive animals were led past. The man in charge was called Cruz, at first a surly individual who clearly resented an imposition which had been arranged at some high level. However, when it came to discussing corn mashes, hay and straw he mellowed and it was clear that we need have no worries on that score. Telling him about the distances we had been covering and the hardships we had all enjoyed together made him look at them with more sympathy, and we left sure that they would be helped to enjoy their well-deserved rest. By now we had also persuaded ourselves that we had earned a treat too, so having returned to Virgen del Camino to tell the Dominicans that we would not be staying after all, we checked into what many point to as the best and most beautiful hotel in the world. Pain, heat and flies serve a useful purpose on travels in providing the contrast required for real luxury to be fully enjoyed. The limited pleasure and relief of cold water needs the occasional counterpoint of a deep, hot soapy bath. Moreover, for the first time on any of our rides I was suffering from heat rashes in uncomfortable places and we all had started filthy colds and were losing our voices. It was time to spoil ourselves.

The Parador of San Marcos was founded in 1168 as a hospital where pilgrims could be looked after by the Knights of St James of the Sword, the main Spanish military religious order. In 1513 it was largely rebuilt and a sublime Renaissance façade 100 metres long was added. Over the elaborately carved main door is a majestic Baroque equestrian figure of Santiago Matamoros riding into battle. Today it is an hotel, another of the excellent establishments run by the Spanish State. Paradors are one of the best things about Spain. Just knowing they are there is enough; it is not necessary to stay in them often or indeed at all. We used them as addresses for our letters en route, for sending and receiving urgent messages via their FAX machines, and we always found them efficient and helpful. Their presence, even for a fleeting visit, reminds me of dropping in to British embassies or consulates in places like Kabul or Manaus in my early travel days. They are there to serve the traveller, and nothing disconcerts them.

We were dusty, our clothes were dirty and we certainly smelt of horse, but our reception was immaculate. 'A suite of two rooms? Of course, Sir. Are you by chance pilgrims? Then there will be a special reduced rate for you. You shall have the two rooms for the price of one.' We sank into luxury and stayed for two nights.

We all loved León Cathedral as much as we disliked the one at Burgos. The best stained glass in Spain was just catching the evening sunshine as we arrived so that the light streamed through the great rose window over the entrance casting multicoloured patterns on the columns of the nave. The purple was so rich and strong that I felt that after 700 years of soaking the stone each day it should have stained it. And up and up above us the columns soared in glorious Gothic striving to reach heaven. Such passion in stone. Carvings everywhere. Faces peering out of every corner and angle: tortured as, being wicked, they are devoured by monstrous beasts or boiled alive in cauldrons licked by the flames of hell; serene and innocent, the faces of children and saints secure in their expectation of heavenly peace. Scallop-shell reminders of the pilgrimage omnipresent in stone, glass and gilt. Endearing heraldic devices on coats of arms made reference to the bearers' association with St James by including the shell, sometimes in unlikely ways. One device was a tree bearing lilies as its flowers and scallops as its leaves.

Outside in the cloister with its carved capitals and frescoes we looked up to see the sun still catching the highest pinnacles. Each was surmounted by a cross or other decoration, save one where a stork's nest rested securely in the cup from which the finial had fallen. Close by, the proud owner stood securely on a cross preening its feathers with its long red beak, a bright splash of colour against the clear azure sky.

Attached to the Parador San Marcos is the church of the same name. Perhaps because this was the spiritual home of the knights of St James, or because every pilgrim would need to refresh his resolve before the last and hardest stage of his journey, the scallop-shell decoration reaches a riotous climax here. There is barely a space which could have a shell on it which lacks one; whole walls of the interior and exterior are covered with serried rows of them. Inside they are mostly gilded, outside plain. They run up the fluting of columns, around the edges of arches, along the eaves and lintels. After making a point of seeking out every scallop along the Way as a talisman and symbol of our pilgrimage, we were now sated, almost as though we had gorged ourselves on a surfeit of Coquilles St Jacques, most culinary of molluscs.

The extraordinary history of the scallop-shell goes far beyond its obscure association with St James. It has appeared in art and sculpture as an object of veneration since at least 400 B.C., the earliest examples being Greek and Roman and relating to Aphrodite or Venus. She was the goddess of beauty and sensual love and was often depicted being born from a shell, most memorably of course by Botticelli. The scallop is a device found throughout architecture, as familiar as the acanthus or the bay-leaf. It was not confined to Europe, occurring in the Middle East and even in the still-undiscovered New World, where it played an important part in the symbolism of many of the pre-Columbian cultures. Here, too, scallops were regularly represented on pottery and in paintings, and they have been found in many graves. In the Yucatan, girls wore scallop-shells as a pubic covering before marriage.

How the Coquille St Jacques became the symbol of St James is unknown. Just like the descriptions of the discovery of the Saint's tomb, the legends of the horseman all date from centuries after the events they describe. Probably it was simply a useful badge to identify those who had made the pilgrimage to Santiago and, being readily available on the surrounding coasts, a convenient one to exploit. The Archbishop of Compostela was given the right by successive Popes to excommunicate anyone who sold scallop-shells to pilgrims anywhere except in the city of Santiago, thereby creating a valuable monopoly.

Between the church and the hotel lies the Chapterhouse, now converted into an excellent small museum housing only objects of exquisite beauty. There are medieval vestments like those we had admired so much in Burgos, fine fragments of sculpture, statuary and ironwork. Several delightful early crosses, bejewelled and beautifully worked, are well displayed, but the star of the show is a small ivory crucifix from the 11th century. It is almost grotesque in its crudeness and lack of sophistication, yet it achieves a spiritual tenderness which holds one rooted to the spot in front of it. Although carved so long ago that it is hard to imagine we have anything in common with those who lived then, it manages to be as modern and moving as anything conceivable from a genius of today.

As I stood before that slender figure which said so much so very simply, I tried to picture what life was really like for its unknown creator's contemporaries. They lived at a time when good and evil were tangible forces which controlled their lives in ways we find hard to conjure up in these days, when life tends to be seen in broadly practical or environmental terms. Sin could be bought off then with indulgences and penances. There were no psychological excuses, just witches to fear and saints to pester for intercession. Heaven and hell, angels and devils, were real and very close in ways which we with first-hand knowledge of space and the composition of matter dismiss as superstition. Yet there was such wisdom in that face, and in evolutionary terms nothing has changed for us over the last few centuries. Much of what I sought was to be revealed to me quite unexpectedly the following morning.

DAY 16 Thursday 24th August   LEÓN

The 12th-century frescoes in the Royal Pantheon of San Isidoro were one of the great sights of my life. As we craned our necks to look at the vaulted ceilings, we were dazzled by the most complete collection of Romanesque painting in the world, largely undamaged, the colours still fresh and untouched by the hand of any subsequent restorer. They have been described as being to Romanesque art what Altamira is to cave painting or the Sistine Chapel is to the Renaissance. As in so many other cases, the main damage done since they were painted was caused by Napoleon's troops, who used the Pantheon as a stable for their cavalry. It was like being transported back nearly a millennium only to find that human beings really were just the same then as now, with similar preoccupations and sense of humour. Their faces are sensitive and acccessible, those of real people. They are going about the daily business of their time, performing chores which are instantly familiar today. The animals and plants are reproduced lovingly and faithfully, revealing characters as alert to what is going on as their owners. Famous for its wit is the handsome brown sheepdog which steals a drink of milk from its master's wooden bowl while he is gazing in amazement at the Angel of the Annunciation. The agricultural tools, the domestic utensils and the weapons are all recognizable and even timeless, since their very practicality makes them satisfactory to use and hard to improve. Only the clothes seem strange for country life, consisting of short woollen tunics which look rather like fashionable cocktail dresses reaching down to the knee or mid-calf. These were worn over thick coloured stockings, which today would be tights, and it crossed my mind to wonder how they kept them up. Garters, I supposed, or were they really early combinations, which would have been much more practical? Finally they wore pointed woollen slippers which could only have given slight protection against thorns, wet and snow in winter. Nonetheless, they all look cheerful and busy so that, for the first time, there in the Pantheon I began seriously to question the premise that life in the Middle Ages was a grindingly grim affair. The evidence of all the splendid buildings from the period proved that when there was peace there must have been an ample surplus to devote to God. The land gave bountifully, having not yet been abused, deforested and polluted; a farmer could probably do quite nicely on his own account when times were good, taxes were low and there was a strong demand for his produce. No wine or beef mountains then! Without succumbing to blind nostalgia which ignores the dangers and discomforts of rural life, it is possible to imagine a world where applying the best of technology to the stable solutions of the past could bring about a very pleasant existence. All that is required is a shift of emphasis from Consumption to Conservation, in all their senses. While the resultant standard of living might be less in crude financial terms, the quality of life would be immeasurably enhanced. Satisfaction does not come only from the accumulation of money, material possessions and the spurious security they give; rather it comes from the real security of living in a stable world where there is mutual support and a desire for continuity rather than change for its own sake. After the headlong dash of the last century, the human race would welcome a period of respite, and the explosion of interest in the natural environment and sustainable systems of life is an indication of this. Handled more in the gentle way of the 12th century than in the brutal manner of the 20th, the world could feed its present population and avoid the famines and the squalor. The model is there in San Isidoro in León.

The calendar of peasant tasks which runs around one of the arches between two of the vaults shows, month by month, the main country chores. Pruning the vines in March and gathering the grapes in September; shaking acorns off the oak tree in October for the pigs, and killing them for winter meat in November; sowing in April, reaping wheat in July, threshing it in August; and finally sitting in front of a blazing fire with a glass of wine on the table, a loaf of bread in one hand and the other raised in benediction for all the good things of life.

We have been beset for so long by propaganda that constant progress towards a materialist ideal is desirable because it liberates man from constant toil. While this is a noble ideal, all too often what it means is that a life of soul-less drudgery is substituted for the cultural diversity which went before and which, for all its faults, was more satisfying than that which replaces it. I know this to be true in the many cases I have seen at first hand of tribal peoples in South America and South-East Asia whose lives are rapidly disrupted by the arrival of well-meaning missionaries and civil servants, let alone the settlers and prospectors who regard them and their economies as grossly inferior. I suspect that the lessons I have learned from observation of what may be termed the Fourth World have much wider application to the apparently hopeless problems of the

Third World. Respecting and endorsing stable and traditional values and slowing the blind pursuit of economic growth and increased productivity might do more for the poor and hungry of the world than all the aid and development projects, which so often do more harm than good.

Two small personal experiences in León that day typified for me the contrast between the two ways of going about things. Louella's camera and my small pocket tape-recorder had both succumbed to the batterings of life in a saddlebag and had stopped working. I was given the name of a man who repaired cameras, tracked him down to his apartment in the old part of the town and showed him how the focusing threads on the lens had jammed. He was interested in what we were doing and for a time we talked about pilgrimage in general and the wonders to be seen in León in particular. He assured me that he would do his best to fix the lens by late afternoon that day, and he subsequently proved as good as his word. I then tracked down the Sanyo agency and repair shop, where a dozen men in white coats worked at well-equipped benches under a huge poster of the sprawling factory buildings of the parent company in Japan. The young man behind the counter wrote down my particulars and said that the repair – the replacement of one small part – would take two weeks. I explained my problem: we were pilgrims on horses who would have to ride on the next morning; I was an author and needed this useful tool of my trade and so on. He exhibited no interest whatever, simply replying, 'Two weeks or buy a new one.'

In the heat of the day, when everything was closing down in León, we drove back towards the east to see the church of San Miguel de Escalada. The winding country lane took us along the valley of the Río Esla through a green small-scale landscape sandwiched between the great dry plains on either side of León. It felt more like being in Brittany than Spain as we passed lush paddocks where dairy cows grazed beneath willow trees.

The church is the finest of all surviving Mozarabic buildings. The Mozarabs were Christians who were permitted to live and worship under the Moors during the latter's occupation of Spain. Judging from the number of Christian churches surviving from those centuries as compared with mosques built by remnant Muslim communities since, it would appear that they were treated much more tolerantly than the eventually triumphant Christians treated their victims. The Mudejares, on the other hand, were Muslims who lived under Christian rule. Significantly, their art is remembered as that executed in architecture, furniture and ironwork in their own designs but mostly for Christian masters.

Apart from revealing much Muslim influence in their style of decoration, the Mozarabs also retained and resurrected some of the

Visigoth traditions which had disappeared when their last Christian kingdom in Spain was conquered in 711. These included the music and text of their own form of Christianity, the Mozarabic rite which survived until the 11th century. The music, which dates from before the Muslim invasion, has sadly been lost because it was written down in a form which once forgotten has remained impossible to decipher. Some of the liturgy is still used, however, including their version of the Lord's Prayer, which is the oldest Christian chant dating from the 4th century. During the Dark Ages there were numerous different Christian churches and sects celebrating in a variety of ways all over Europe, such as the Celtic, Visigothic, Gallican, Arian and Priscillian. As late as 1085 a duel was fought at Toledo to decide whether the Latin or Mozarabic rite should be used. The Mozarabic champion won there, but by the end of that century the Roman church had won the dogmatic war and then set about systematically discrediting all reference to previous Christian philosophies, branding them as heresies and eliminating as far as possible all reference to them. Knowing this makes the Dark Ages seem much less dark.

The church of San Miguel de Escalada was built in the year 913 as part of a now vanished 9th-century monastery. It has been well restored quite recently, so that it looks much as it must have done when the tower and extraordinary exterior gallery were added in 1050. The lines of the building are clean and pure, there is marble everywhere – warm where the sun strikes the satisfying horseshoe arches of the gallery, cool inside where the light is filtered through alabaster windows to suffuse the bare interior. The church stands by itself in empty countryside, and we were let in by a guardian who then left us alone. The peace and silence were absolute; it felt as though they had never been disturbed during the past millennium. There were none of the echoes of destruction and discord which disturb most other ecclesiastical buildings in Spain and we all, even Merlin, talked in whispers while inside. There was no furniture, no chairs, no altar, no screen, but there was plenty to see. Carved stone panels and the capitals of columns bore pictures which revealed the origins of their sculptors. A row of elegant birds probed at bunches of grapes, pecked seeds and preened their feathers. Representing living creatures they would have to be Mozarabic, since this is forbidden to Islamic artists. They achieved their equally delightful effects on the capitals and arches, where their exuberant fancy conjured foliage and geometrical devices into flowing Mudejar patterns.

DAY 17 Friday 25th August
LEÓN TO SAN FELIZ/HOSPITAL DE ORBIGO

As we rode along the main road out of León, facing the oncoming traffic and, as usual, with Louella leading, a flock of sheep suddenly started up just to our left across a ditch. Guadalquivir shied out into the road, panicked and began to prance about uncontrollably. Mercifully there was no vehicle passing at that instant and Duque did not join in and follow him; but it was a very busy road and I could do nothing but watch helplessly as Louella regained control, continued across to the far side, waved down the traffic now overtaking her, cantered along with it for a hundred metres and then was able to stop and dismount. When another gap in the flow of vehicles allowed me to rejoin her, we were both shaking at the unexpectedness of her narrow escape and, although it never happened again, we were always a little tense inside when it was necessary to follow busy roads. Unfortunately, for the rest of that day the Way hugged the main N120 and we were seldom able to escape into the fields alongside. As a result we passed the next hours rather miserably, rather than delay to see the villages we passed.

Our reward was the marvellous long, narrow, stone bridge over the Río Orbigo. The most impressive of pilgrim bridges, it has twenty arches and continues to span what must once have been dangerous marshes on either side of the river itself. It is also the setting of one of the most romantic incidents in Spanish history, the story of which may have inspired Cervantes to create Don Quixote, the ultimate parody of the chivalrous knight errant. In 1434 one Don Suero de Quiñones, driven to distraction by love for a lady who scorned his advances, somehow managed to persuade nine other knights to join him in challenging all comers to joust with them. As it was a Holy Year – that is one on which St James's Day, July 25th, fell on a Sunday – and the challenge was issued on July 10th, there was no shortage of takers and the fighting continued for thirty days. Many were injured on what came to be known as *el paso honoroso* but there was only one death. When he had vanquished all, Don Suero felt able to remove the iron collar he had vowed to wear until his gesture was made and go to Compostela himself, where he offered St James a golden bracelet in thanksgiving. Whether he won the lady in the end, history does not relate.

Waiting for us on the bridge were our leaping, waving ground crew who had found a field for us to camp in beyond the town itself, in a hamlet called San Feliz. And a happy, friendly place it turned out to be. Joan had made friends with one of the families and they let us hose down our hot horses, a treat they much enjoyed. They also pressed on us armfuls of fresh-mown hay from their loft. Putting up our tents and making sure the horses were tethered safely with plenty to eat took no time, so that we were able to drive on into Astorga which we would be passing through the following morning.

What we wanted to see there was the bishop's palace built by the most remarkable of art nouveau architects, Antonio Gaudi. His best-known work is the incredible unfinished Church of the Holy Family in Barcelona, which George Orwell described as one of the most hideous buildings in the world. Although Gaudi worked on it for forty-three years until his untimely death when he was run over by a tram in 1926, he left no plans and ever since controversy has raged as to whether it should be finished or left as a memorial to him. His palace in Astorga is on an altogether smaller scale, and we instantly fell under its spell. It is a happy extravaganza, yet constructed with such flair and vitality that there is nothing cheap or vulgar about it. A fantasy medieval castle, which from outside looks like a doll's house yet is spacious within, having grand staircases, stained-glass windows, statues and paintings. A gallimaufry of styles and materials, it achieves a unity through the strength of character and purpose of its deeply religious creator. Louella announced that, transported into the countryside, it would be her dream house. That is, she added, if we ever had to leave Maidenwell, which I had thought was quite eccentric enough for anyone's taste. I was surprised by her enthusiasm as it really is a most impractical and peculiar dwelling, but the attraction of art nouveau is very sudden and personal. It was exciting to see her sharing my own far from fully developed passion for its bizarre style.

The exhibitions inside the palace, which comprise a Museum of the Way, were not very impressive. It was the building itself which kept drawing our eyes away from the objects on display. These included wooden sculptures of St James from the 13th century onwards; I realized that the 17th-century figure of St James which I have at home was a better example than any of them. He has a gentle, rather elongated face and posture, which is reminiscent of El Greco. He seemed to have entered my life in all sorts of unexpected ways without my being aware of it. I even have a dreadfully bad gilded representation of a scallop designed by Salvador Dali and reproduced as the trophy given to recipients of the Krug Award for Excellence. Awarded for only one year (1980), they went to such distinguished people as Olivier and Gielgud (Theatre), Nureyev (Ballet) and Graham Greene (Literature). My category was 'Adventure and Discovery'.

Once more, as in León, the sun was setting as we visited the cathedral across the square from Gaudi's palace. Again the evening light enhanced a feature to lift it above the simply beautiful. This time it was not the way it streamed through the stained glass, but the extraordinary fashion in which it softened and brought alive the rose limestone of the western façade. Carved relief figures of Renaissance angels and saints looked their best in the last of the sunshine, and in the centre over the door was St James in his most gentle guise, gathering his cloak around him and stepping out as a pilgrim. You can never escape him on the pilgrimage; he is always there in various costumes waiting to greet pilgrims at the end of their day's travel.

DAY 18 Saturday 26th August
                    SAN FELIZ TO RABANAL DEL CAMINO

A kind Augustinian priest, who was visiting his family in the village, came to call on us during the evening. He said he owned a wood a short distance away where there was plenty of grass, and suggested we moved the horses there. As we walked together through the darkness he told me he had spent his life working with tribal people in different parts of the world. He had lived at Iquitos on the Amazon ministering to the Indians there; more recently he had been in the Philippines with the hill tribes working for Cardinal Sin whom he knew well. He was an old man and it was too late to begin a discussion which might well last until dawn if once it got going, so I expressed polite interest but resisted the temptation to tell him about my own involvement in such matters. Instead I listened carefully as he gave me directions for a cross-country route to Astorga, avoiding all roads.

This led through holm-oak woods and over a series of ridges networked with tracks. Lovely country to ride through but frustratingly impenetrable when lost, as we were within half an hour. One path after another petered out, when we would force our way on in the same direction until reaching open country again. Sometimes we saw figures working patches of cultivated land, guiding a single plough behind a draught horse, but they were always far away while the route ahead looked promising and at the time it never seemed worth making a wide detour to ask the way. Then, once lost again, we would kick ourselves for not doing so. We came on wide firebreaks bulldozed through the woods, which we followed hopefully until they curved back the way we had come. Irrevocably we were drawn back to the road which, once we gave up trying to head across country, soon led us out of the woods and on to a high plateau. Almost at once we saw a yellow arrow indicating that we could leave the road again and follow the well-marked normal route. This soon brought us to the edge of the escarpment, from where we had a magnificent prospect out over Astorga in the valley below us and across to the hills beyond which would in due course become Galicia. The plains of Castile were behind us and the last stretch lay ahead. There was a tall granite cross with a carved top at the most prominent spot; it commemorated Toribio, a 5th-century bishop who was reputedly chased out of Astorga by a population unwilling to be converted by him. At this place he stopped for a last look and shook the dust from his feet to show symbolically that he would not be returning. Doubtless he quoted St Matthew x 14 into the wind: 'And whosoever shall not receive you, nor hear your words, when ye depart out of that house or city, shake off the dust of your feet.'

Heading in the opposite direction, we rode through the centre of the town and out the other side without mishap to find the countryside becoming more and more attractive and interesting with every mile we covered. This was the country of the Maragatos, obscure people who may have some odd ethnic origin (being a tribe who once settled here in the dim past), or may simply be an enclave of local people who have remained peculiarly attached to their traditions. One who believed in their extreme oddity was George Borrow, author of *The Bible in Spain*, written following four astonishing journeys made between 1835 and 1839 which covered a large part of the Iberian peninsula, and during which he attempted fairly unsuccessfully to distribute copies of the New Testament. He describes the Maragatos as:

... perhaps the most singular cast to be found amongst the chequered population of Spain. They have their own peculiar customs and dress, and never intermarry with the Spaniards. Their name is a clue to their origin, as it signifies 'Moorish Goths', and at the present day their garb differs but little from that of the Moors of Barbary, as it consists of a long tight jacket, secured at the waist by a broad girdle, loose short trousers which terminate at the knee, and boots and gaiters. Their heads are shaven, a slight fringe of hair being only left at the lower part.

These costumes are now only worn at fiestas or weddings, and the source of their legendary wealth has also dried up. They used to be the most trusted and expensive muleteers in the country, 'almost the entire commerce of nearly one half of Spain' passing through their hands, again according to Borrow. Today their villages lie partly in ruins, mostly abandoned, their thatched roofs crumbling. Very picturesque to ride through, but sad since the land is poor and there is little to attract people back to it. Wild sweeping purple heather moorland, with only occasional clumps of oak and fertile spots in the valleys, leads up into and over the rugged windswept mountains of León. The people who were still living in the villages we passed through were hospitable, offering us water which, when we accepted it for the horses in Santa Catalina de Somoza, was brought out from the courtyard in a bucket. The elderly couple there told us that it had been an extraordinarily busy year because of the Pope, and that more than 400 pilgrims a day had gone by their house some weeks before, but now it was over and they hardly ever saw anyone. From here on we were much troubled by horseflies which settled out of our sight below the horses' necks or on their legs and drove them mad. Riding became difficult as they threw themselves about in efforts to dislodge the inch-long insects which were sucking their blood. Their *mosqueros* protected their faces and we were constantly slapping those we could see, but there were always more. Normally they did not pay too much attention to horseflies, but this area must produce especially painful ones. Occasionally one would settle on our bare arms or even bite through the back of our shirts, and we would learn for ourselves why the horses minded so much.

After 20 kilometres we reached Rabanal del Camino, the village where the Confraternity of Saint James in London is planning to restore a ruined former hospice for pilgrims. Rabanal is a lovely place with a tiny population, who had all been won over to our side by Joan and Merlin's groundwork before our arrival. The key figure in the community is Chonina, the energetic widow who runs the local bar with the help of her son Miguel Angel. She said that we could put the horses in one of her fields, though we would not be able to camp there as the track to it was impossible for vehicles. She had recently done up two rooms above her bar, and she showed them to us. They were spotless, as were the *servicios* downstairs next to the bar, so we decided to stay there rather than put up the tents. The field was by far the best yet, with succulent herbage growing around a muddy spring. It was the first green grass field our horses had been in, and surrounded by a crumbling stone wall which I repaired so that they could graze without being tethered. They put their heads down as soon as we released them.

Miguel Angel had eight milch cows and no shortage of places to graze them. There was water everywhere, running in little rivulets down into the narrow streets of the village and held in brimming drinking troughs. Rabanal must once have been a prosperous place, and it was sad to see how many of the houses had roofs which were desperately in need of repair. We had seen virtually no houses being restored sympathetically along the Way; it seemed to us that either they were allowed to fall down or they were replaced with modern monstrosities. We saw few tilers and no thatchers at work, although these are still a quite familiar sight in the English countryside. Perhaps this is because thatching costs a lot more than corrugated iron, and there is neither the money available, from property speculation, nor are there planning laws requiring buildings and villages to retain their original character. Only those buying second homes in the country could afford to restore properly, and their arrival tends to undermine the community spirit. It is nonetheless a pity that, at least on the Way of St James which is travelled and admired by so many pilgrims, there should not be more incentives to builders and restorers to observe a standard which would not destroy the look of the villages, and preferably to restore rather than replace. The plans for the rebuilding of Rabanal's hospice look like a model, and perhaps this example will be followed before it is too late. The red pantile roof will be mended, the crumbling walls repaired and extended; there will be bunk beds, showers and an attractive patio with a balcony and tables where pilgrims can sit and relax in peace.

We climbed up the rickety church tower which overlooks the hospice, the cluster of red village roofs and the wild blue empty country beyond. As the evening shadows lengthened, cows were driven across the square by Chonina's café and into a building for the night. Much later, long after dark, a large flock of sheep and goats returned to the village and they too were put indoors for safety. From what, we wondered? Surely there was no longer any danger from wolves here? Perhaps they were prone to wandering, or there were rustlers; perhaps some had to be milked, perhaps it was just the way it had always been done. Later, in Galicia, we were to see securely fenced fields where cows grazed safely and contentedly, but were still watched over by old people although there was no danger that they would stray or be disturbed. It is not easy to get closer to the Middle Ages than in remote rural Spain, where custom dies hard and there is great satisfaction and security to be derived from observing tradition and watching over domestic animals.

Also living in Rabanal for the summer and studying the origins of the pilgrimage was a Swiss anthropologist, Barbara Haab, with whom we were able to speak briefly. She had chosen an ideal place to base herself; integrated happily with the local population, yet with a constant stream of pilgrims to question on their motives and experiences. Chonina, too, has kept a scrapbook about the pilgrimage and, when we had finished our bowls of her legendary garlic-laced pilgrim soup, we looked through it with her in the now crowded bar where most of the villagers had congregated. There were entries by and references to many of the people we had met or read about in our preparation for our journey. Laurie Dennett, the Canadian woman who walked alone and on foot from Chartres to Santiago in 1986, raising a large sum of money for multiple sclerosis research, was there; she had written affectionately about Chonina in her subsequent book *A Hug for the Apostle*, but no copy had yet reached Rabanal and I promised I would see that this was remedied. A man whom we had met in the Camargue before we set out on our French ride, the famous Homme à Cheval, advertised in Chonina's book in 1983 that he would take a group of riders from Jaca to Compostela in 19 days. This seemed excessively fast, as Jaca was about as far back in the Pyrenees as Roncesvalles and we had now been riding for 18 days with at least another week to go. Nevertheless it was good to feel ourselves being carried along on a tide of energy by so many other recent pilgrims that failure now seemed out of the question, and we went up to our neat beds feeling much more confident and optimistic about what lay ahead.

DAY 19 Sunday 27th August   **RABANAL TO CACABELOS**

*U*p in the mountains it was gloriously cool with a light breeze even though the sun shone in a cloudless turquoise sky, which must have been making life unbearably hot down in the plains behind us. Foncebadón was an apparently abandoned village but we came on a surprising amount of activity there. A truck was parked near the ruined church, and a rough-looking lot of shepherds were rounding up all the animals from the surrounding hills with their dogs and driving them towards it. Perhaps, we thought, they were stealing them after all and life was not as peaceful as it seemed. More sinister was a German whose parked car we had passed before leaving the road and who was inspecting the houses with a couple of important-looking men in suits. This, we decided, was a speculator come to buy the whole village and turn it into a holiday camp. A more remote and derelict place it would be hard to find, although the panoramas in all directions were uninterrupted and breathtaking. Every single house was dilapidated and falling down, though most of the roofs were still just in place. They had been made of slate, not thatch, and the atmosphere was quite different from cosy fertile Rabanal 6 kilometres and 1,000 feet (300m) back down behind us. Exposed to the elements at nearly 5,000 feet (1,500m) above sea level, Foncebadón must always have been a hard place to live, although it was once an important stopping place on the Way with an inn, a hospital for pilgrims and special royal privileges. Now it is almost self-consciously picturesque in its desolation and clearly beyond natural redemption. We just hoped as we picked our way through the rubble of the only street that whatever the future held, nothing too out of keeping with the spirit of this wild and wonderful stretch of the pilgrim Way would be created. Larks sang above the open hillsides and we pressed cheerfully on up to the top until we reached the celebrated Cruz de Ferro, the iron cross attached to a long wooden stake and stuck in a great *montjoie* or heap of stones. The word *montjoie* is a corruption of Mons Jovis or Mount of Jupiter, the old name for the stone cairns which today still mark routes across wild and uninhabited places. I have followed them in the Sahara and Gobi deserts, as well as on the Massif Central in France and indeed at the top of Scafell in the Lake District. Once whole chains of *montjoies* may have marked the pilgrim routes across Europe to Santiago; now this is one of the few to survive. Deep snow makes this pass virtually impassable in winter weather, and the villagers from the scattered settlements around used to be freed from taxes if they marked the route with long stakes. Even in August there was a chill in the air as we dismounted to add our stones to the pile and rest the horses after their climb. Ahead lay range after range of mountains, but we would never be higher than this again; in fact it was the highest point since the high Pyrenees beyond Roncesvalles. From here the road wound down and down in a series of wide loops, the Way cutting corners and leading us along delightful stony tracks through clumps of heather, broom and gorse between which grew beds of purple autumn crocus. Much of the time we walked, leading the horses down steep scrambles and enjoying stretching our legs. At other times there were level ridges along which we could canter, and always the pleasure of being back in the mountains after those endless plains and flat horizons. Now there were enticing deep valleys where wooded slopes and steep hillsides of scrub tempted us to make detours and explore the shady ravines and rivers which must lie below. Instead we forged on and in time dropped down into El Acebo (The Holly), one of the prettiest and best known villages with a narrow main street winding between slate-roofed houses whose decorative balconies overhang it. Although these were almost all deserted and shuttered, there were several people in gardens and on terraces away from the road, giving us the impression (since it was Sunday) that perhaps they are being used as second homes. This might not be such a bad thing, if only there were laws which protected villages like El Acebo from modern intrusions but required people to restore or rebuild in a sympathetic style. Such, however, seems not to be the case in Spain, and we were to see some ghastly modern eyesores disfiguring perfectly designed and proportioned streets both in towns and in remote villages.

Another 2,000 feet (600m) descent, well marked and across country but steep and stony, brought us to Molinaseca to find a delightful cool pellucid bathing place in the Río Meruelo where it passes under a Roman bridge, over which we rode and where we met the others for a picnic. It was all too neat and municipal around the pool for us to tether the horses; the grass was mown and there were benches and flower-beds. Guided by some small boys, we led the horses back up-stream to a place in a poplar wood where there were mill-streams and long grass. There we left them tied on their long ropes to separate trees, their saddles and other tack piled beside them. We still felt ourselves sufficiently far from civilization not to fear theft too much. The water was icy-cold as we plunged in, very refreshing and above all absolutely clean, the first such river we had met in Spain. A pity, but at least it showed what could be done if the will was there.

The approach to Ponferrada a few miles further on that afternoon provided a dramatic contrast with the cleanliness and civic pride of Molinaseca. The attractive village of Campo, with its narrow picturesque alleys, is now almost a suburb of the big industrial town whose factories threaten to engulf it. The open area between city and village is largely taken up by one of the smelliest rubbish-tips we were to pass, which we did as fast as we could – entering the town not by the iron bridge, built in the 12th century for pilgrims after which it is named, but by the medieval stone bridge called Mascaron, meaning 'large mask', for no reason I have been able to fathom. Quickly lost in the maze of streets around the centre and made nervous by the dangerous way our horses slipped on the smooth asphalt, we stopped to ask the way of some young men who proved to be very drunk. All they were capable of was making cowboy noises, but their misdirections brought us to the Templar Castle, founded in 1119 and recently much restored. We rode along the embankment below the crenellated walls, battlements and round towers feeling romantic, although there was no one else there to see us.

We had a predictably horrible time negotiating the western sub-urbs of Ponferrada, through which high-speed main roads now run. Then suddenly we were back in Arcadia, where fast-flowing canals irrigated fruitful gardens, where we were able to pluck apples and plums from overhanging branches and where amiable peasants greeted us with smiles and an occasional '*Hola, peregrinos*' as they wheeled giant pumpkins home on overflowing wheelbarrows. Water troughs and drinking places abounded for the horses and we let them have their fill as they were tired; we too were able to pause for a stirrup cup or two in the tranquil villages we passed through where, as so often happens in Spain, time seemed to stand still in spite of the proximity of a major industrial city.

Joan had said she would try to find us somewhere to camp in this landscape, which had looked promising even on our maps. Our rendezvous was the point where the Way crossed the main road shortly before Cacabelos. As we were about to ride across, disappointed that she and Merlin were not there to meet us although it was now quite late in the evening, a car drove out of the lane opposite. (A yellow arrow on a stone indicated that that was the route for pilgrims to follow.) The car stopped, a couple got out, opened the boot, lifted out a large shopping-bag overflowing with rubbish . . . and tipped it into the hedge. They then went back to their car and drove off. We watched aghast, too surprised to do or say anything; and we would probably have been regarded as mad had we done so. In England I would have ridden in front of the car and demanded that they clear it up; but this was not my country, and my Spanish was not up to the subtleties of the argument which would follow. It was one of the most blatant examples of why Spain is covered in rubbish and, after we had crossed the road, we went over to look at the disgusting heap of waste food, old clothes, plastic and tins. 'Look!' said Louella, who was if possible even more angry and shocked than I was. 'Some of the paper has blown up into the hedge already.' Sure enough a large piece of orange cardboard was lodged in a tree beside the road. 'No, it's tied on with string,' I said. 'That's odd.' We fetched it down and saw that it was a note which otherwise we would certainly have missed. 'Hopeless here,' it read, 'have had to go to the camp-site 1 km beyond Cacabelos on the right; Joan and Merlin.'

In a lifetime of travelling all over the world by almost every known means, I do not recall ever staying in an official camp-site. The idea has always repelled me, representing the antithesis of what I regard as proper travel. Of course in Amazonas and the jungles of Borneo, in African and Chinese deserts, there were no camp-sites, but in Europe or wherever else such places existed I would instinctively seek out somewhere as private and remote as possible. I was dimly aware that 'wild' camping was becoming increasingly difficult, at least in the Western world, and from time to time I had vaguely wondered why more people did not simply ask farmers for permission to camp in their fields, as we had done on both our European rides. In thirty years no one has ever asked permission to camp on my Cornish farm, and I had felt sorry for all the campers who came to Cornwall and missed the pleasure and excitement which were there for the asking. It seemed such a pity that they had to go to those 'awful' camp-sites with all those 'awful' other people. Nothing would ever get me into one, I had thought. After reading Joan's note, we groaned both at the prospect of having to go further at the end of a long day and at the appalling idea that we would be paying to camp with other people.

Cacabelos was unexpectedly delightful, our guidebooks having barely mentioned it, with charming metal and wooden balconies along the streets and a cool colonnaded central square, yet with green countryside glimpsed up alleyways on all sides. We were still on the route of Sir John Moore's retreat, although it then being midwinter his troops had gone around the mountains since they were covered in snow, rather than over them as we had done. Here at Cacabelos they had engaged the French and the gallant 15th once again distinguished themselves, holding the enemy in check for more than twenty-four hours while the rest of the army escaped. During fierce hand-to-hand fighting in the Plaza one of the Hussars decapitated a French chasseur with a single blow of his sabre.

I wanted to linger instead of having to hurry through and my determination to dislike where we were going deepened. Crossing the Río Cua by the road bridge we turned right, passed an interesting ruined building called the Santuario de la Quinta Angustia (the Sanctuary of the Fifth Anguish) – anything rather than an official camp-site, I muttered – and on down a leafy lane beside the river.

El Humerol Camping, when we arrived there, had lush green grass and thick clover under the poplar trees which defined the camping spaces. Our horses badly needed some good grazing as we had no more hay with us then (we usually had a spare bale on the roof-rack). But better still was to come. The tents stood four square beside the car; for once the ground was perfect for hammering in tent-pegs. 'There are hot showers, clean loos, a hosepipe with water for the horses and a nice bar with cold drinks,' said Joan. It seemed like heaven, and being the end of the season there was hardly anyone else there. I viewed the French family 50 yards away, sitting at a camp table eating their supper, with deep suspicion. But they shamed me instantly by being perfectly charming, their teenage daughters rushing over to pet the horses. Suddenly the idea of staying in a camp-site, far from being undesirable, became highly to be sought after. Why camp on stony, uneven ground and make do with a rub-down with a damp flannel, when all this could be ours for a miniscule charge? Why condemn the horses to a bucketful of water from a dirty stream, when they could have unlimited quantities from a hosepipe? Camp-sites were transformed overnight into ideal homes for us and our steeds, preferable in many ways to hotels, even, as we could sleep beside the horses and keep an eye on them.

As we tucked in to the hot meat and vegetables Joan had prepared with unusual ease – after slices of melon first and Petit Suisse with cheese to follow – I announced that in future she should seek out camp-sites as our first choice since they were close to heaven. Thus are the principles of a lifetime overturned in minutes. However, none thereafter permitted horses in spite of all Joan's powers of persuasion, and so I have been allowed to retain my illusions about them.

GALICIA

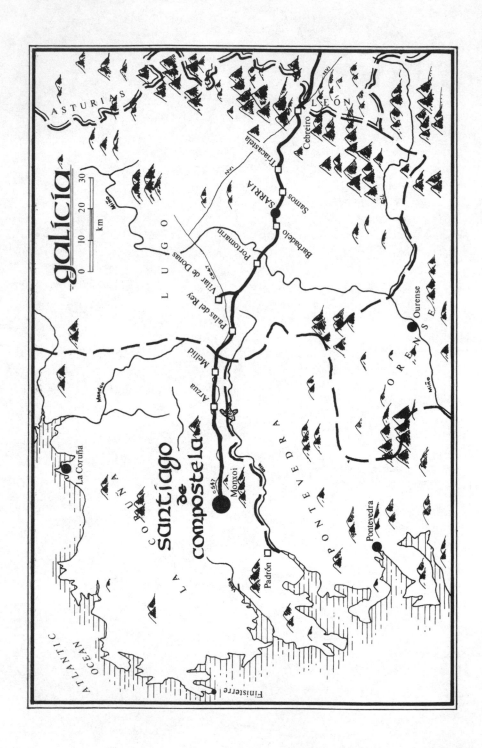

We managed to stay off the road all the way between Caca-belos and Villafranca del Bierzo, although the guides and yellow arrows all lead along it. An old couple of whom we asked the way when cutting across country as we set off, assured us that this would be possible, and that we would in fact be following the old, original and almost forgotten Camino Real. Sometimes there was a clear track alongside an overgrown hedge, but then we would have to meander through new vineyards which interrupted it until we saw someone else to direct us. All we met were pleased and indeed proud to do so, claiming that the official route had unfairly bypassed them. Valtuille de Arriba was an especially pretty place, a village fixed in time which alone made worthwhile the inconvenience of having to stop and ask the way so often. The houses were wonder-fully rustic with crumbling external staircases under which firewood was stored. This was just the sort of place, we felt, which might still use the traditional beehives of the region; these were made from hollowed tree-trunks, with a slate placed on the top. There is a story which Robert Southey tells, fortunately not in verse this time, of an English traveller who needing to relieve himself one moonlit night, goes behind an inn near here and seeing one, 'congratulated himself that the people were so advanced as to have made such a convenience. . .and was in a situation very unfit for making a speedy retreat when he took off the cover, and out came the bees upon him.'

Villafranca del Bierzo, like the other Villafrancas along the Spanish Way, was founded in the 11th century by French settlers and is the largest and best known of all such settlements. With what has been described as possibly the longest and steepest ascent of the journey ahead of us, and with most of the morning already gone, we were anxious to press on. It was a lovely town with narrow cobbled streets overhung by more wrought-iron balconies and fine stone coats of arms. There are churches and castles where one day I hope to return and linger.

We paused at the church of Santiago as we led the horses down the steep descent into town. Here at the battered Romanesque Puerta del Perdón it was possible for exhausted pilgrims – if they received a certificate endorsing their inability to continue – to be granted absolution without the need to continue to Santiago de Compostela. It seems that the tradition continues but we were in no mood to find out if this were true, feeling fit and eager to enter Galicia at last. We even took the advice of a returning Spanish pilgrim we met at the church to follow another alternative route after the town, one which would take us high above the road along the ridge of the Cerro del Real far from people and traffic. It was good advice, although the first part of the climb was so steep and stony that we wondered for a time if we were wise to have taken it. Then we reached the first point from which we could look down on Villafranca dominated by its 15th-century castle with stubby round towers at each corner. These were apparently destroyed by the British army during the Napoleonic wars. From then on both the views and the terrain became better and better. Far, far below us traffic beetled along the black asphalt road winding up the valley of the Río Valcarce.

Once it was level enough to mount again we passed through the shoulder-high broom easily, plucking fat blackberries off the brambles. High up there were surprisingly robust pine woods where we rested in the welcome shade and looked across the valley to the wild uninhabited hills opposite. Later the woods were of Spanish chestnut, venerable trees which transformed our surroundings to the medieval forests where knights rode in search of dragons. There was no water along the ridge, so before descending we made a short detour to an unmarked village called Pradela – another which seemed almost unaware of the outside world and unused to travellers. The roofs were of coarse slate, scalloped like a fish's fins and covering the chimneys as well. The little church was quite different from anything we had seen en route, slate-roofed again and Celtic in feeling, but with a pierced bell-tower just like the one we had last seen at San Juan de Ortega on the far side of Burgos. The villagers were shy and uncommunicative, but there was a good water-trough and we continued refreshed. An hour of steep and slippery descent to the valley floor was followed by some miles along the old road, which for long stretches had fortunately survived the arrival of its high-speed replacement. It led us through a series of pretty and prosperous villages with strange names, Ambasmestas, Ambascasas, Ruitelan, to Herrerias where in ancient times, as its name indicates, there were iron foundries.

The 17th-century Italian pilgrim priest, Domenico Laffi, was impressed by the size of the water-driven tilt hammers used to work the metal, but we had neither time nor need to find out if any still plied their trade there or had converted to shoeing horses. We did notice an interesting field pattern between the village and the river where narrow strips of land were divided by rows of stakes, giving the impression that perhaps they were farmed communally as water meadows; these would have required a sophisticated management of the river in order to flood them at certain seasons and so greatly increase their productivity. Certainly they looked wonderfully lush

and tempting to us as grazing for the horses, but we still had a
mountain to climb that day.

The up-stream end of the village of Herrerias is known as the
Hospital Inglés, presumably because of some long-forgotten English
connection. This is first referred to in a dispensation given by Pope
Alexander III in 1178, where it is also stated that pilgrims used to
be buried in the church, but there is little trace of anything today.

Shortly afterwards we left the river bank and entered a quite
different world of precipitous narrow high-banked lanes down which
water and mud trickled over the bare rock and giant cobblestones.
At times these were shaped and set in the ground, though mostly
disarranged, and we realized that we were following what may have
been – before it became a pilgrim route – a Roman road. It was
cool and pleasant under the overhanging trees and bushes, so that
we felt ourselves back in Cornwall, where exactly comparable green
lanes lead off the edge of Bodmin Moor, some passing through our
own farm. Bracken and brambles crowded the hedges, smaller ferns
grew on wet banks and only the acacia confirmed that we were
further south.

Every now and then we met herds of brown and beige milch cows
being driven by ruddy-faced farmers in cloth caps who would have
blended inconspicuously in any Cornish market. Their villages were
now unmistakably Celtic too, granite and slate with moss on the
roofs and green lichen on the walls. However, it was not until we
were again in the open on another high ridge that we came to the
milestone informing us that we were now entering Galicia at last. It
was brightly painted with various coats of arms, and made us feel
welcome to the last province on the Way. Soon after we were within
hailing distance of Cebreiro and our ground crew, who had come
round by road and arranged that we could stay in the hostel, all
sharing one small room. Right next to the 9th- and 10th-century
church, the oldest complete church on the pilgrim Way, it was built
from the ruins of the original 7th-century monastic hospital for
pilgrims. Founded by Count Giraldo de Aurillac and still bearing
his sanctified name, it continued as a Benedictine monastery until
1854. As we rode up we saw an elderly priest with a crutch walking
slowly along the road. This, we knew, must be the famous Don
Elias, prime author of the guide which had accompanied us all the
way and proved so invaluable with its detailed maps. Earlier in the
year he had been very ill in hospital and I had not been able to call
on him. It was good to see that he had survived but, sadly, we were
to learn later of his death in the following December, aged only
sixty. During his lifetime he had done more than anyone else to
restore interest in the Way and, indeed, personally to explore it and
mark the best routes. A shy and modest man, he greeted us civilly

and said that we could graze our horses overnight in the bare enclosure beside the inn. This was already occupied by a flock of sheep, a huge Pyrenean mountain dog which barked incessantly, an old man raking firewood towards the cellars and two Englishwomen in a tent. These last were there to study the other celebrated feature of Cebreiro, the village of *pallozas* – prehistoric dwellings of stone and thatch which were occupied by locals until quite recently and have been preserved largely as tourist objects and pilgrim refuges, but also as extremely interesting archaeological relics.

I would like to have had time to pick the ladies' brains about the building's significance, but with horses there is always much to do before one can relax. By the time they had been settled and fed the remains of our hay and corn, we were out of both and I had to set off in the car in search of more.

Down below Cebreiro in the village of Pedrafita, which lies on the main road, I tracked down a flour-mill. It looked just like any other stone two-storey house, but behind the wooden garage doors was a traditional mill where fibre sacks of wheat, oats and barley were stacked in an atmosphere thick with flour and cobwebs. Flights of wooden steps led to the higher levels and when I gave my prescription for horse feed the miller scurried up and down them with heavy sacks across his shoulders which he mixed and graded until we were both satisfied. He was a cheerful round-faced man, a caricature of the jolly miller, his face powdered white, and he was refreshingly curious about what we were doing. It being his business, he allowed me to pay a fair price for the two sacks I bought from him; but with a daughter who was a nurse in England and being interested himself in horses, I was not allowed to leave until we had exhausted my Spanish on the subject of travel.

It was dark by the time I reached Cebreiro again and I could see a light in the church. There I found Louella and Merlin lighting candles for all their relations and friends at home. They had fifteen flickering merrily in front of the 12th-century Madonna and were sitting quietly together. There is always so much happening on a journey such as we were on – so many people to talk to, so many things which have to be done, so far to go each day – that sometimes we forgot how good it was just to be still for a while. I joined them and we looked up at the gently smiling figures, the mother's head tilted a little forward, reputedly inclined in recognition of the miracle which took place at Cebreiro. A doubting monk giving communion to a faithful peasant who had struggled through a storm to receive it – and secretly despising him for having bothered to do so – was astonished when the bread and wine turned to flesh and blood before his eyes. This simple story of manifest transubstantiation seems to have swept across Europe, carried by returning pilgrims to be woven into all manner of medieval tales from the search for the Holy Grail to the origins of Wagner's *Parsifal*. The touchingly simple gold and silver chalice in which this miracle occurred, and which many believed actually to be the Holy Grail, is preserved in the church – rather insecurely, we thought, in view of the number of people who have been searching for it down the ages. In Celtic legend, the Holy Grail or Sangrail was the cup used by Christ in the Last Supper, or that in which Joseph of Arimathaea collected some of His blood at the Crucifixion and which he then brought to Glastonbury – or both. The Quests of the Knights of the Round Table were in search of it, and normally doomed to failure since it disappeared if approached by anyone not of perfect purity – which perhaps is why the chalice at Cebreiro is safe after all.

We dined in the hostel amply if not elegantly on *sopa de fideos* – the Spanish national dish of noodle soup – followed by hake, potatoes and fruit, all served by Don Elias's bumptious young nephew who larked about with Merlin, picking him up by his neck and creating chaos. He was so good-natured that it was impossible to be cross with him, even when he grabbed the plates while we were still eating and whistled through his teeth as he served us. But it was a relief when he left us to our coffee. We were joined by the only other guest, a big-bearded white-haired man who brought over a bottle of Cointreau and began to talk about his country Galicia. Dropping with sleep I listened intently, realizing as the evening wore on that I was being treated to a rare monologue by someone who had original ideas on everything but knew what he was talking about. The girls left us to it, and in the morning only fragments remained in my memory.

'There is no bullring in the whole of Galicia,' my friend told me. 'This is a very different place from the rest of Spain. It is a matriarchy and women still hold many of the important posts and most of the power behind the scenes.' I already knew that this autonomous part of Spain was Celtic in most respects apart from the language, consisting of wild wet mountainous country leading to a broken Atlantic coastline with innumerable harbours and sandy beaches. I had not realized how important fishing was to the province's economy. 'Vigo is the biggest fishing port in Europe,' he told me proudly, 'and Spain's fishing fleet, which is mostly based in Galicia, is the third largest in the world, after Russia and Japan.' The bad news is that, as a result of this, Galicia is fast becoming the main entry point for drugs coming into Europe. They are dropped off out in the Atlantic and then distributed by the freezer trucks.

Being from A Coruña himself (Corunna in English, La Coruña in Castilian) he resented the fact that Santiago with only a third of its population had been made the provincial capital. Even the usually impeccable Michelin *Green Guide* and the *Encyclopaedia Britannica* cite La Coruña as the capital of Galicia, but they are wrong. 'If you are born in front of the sea you have a wider horizon than those inland,' he quoted passionately, as we worked our way down the bottle.

On pilgrimages and crusades he became even more passionate. 'Of course the bones at Compostela are not those of St James at all!' he asserted. 'They belong to Priscillian of Avila. He was the 4th-century bishop who became the first Christian to be executed for heresy. Interested in sorcery, he was accused of taking part in fertility rites, rain-making ceremonies and sexual orgies. In Galicia we venerated him as a martyr. His body was brought back and buried somewhere near Compostela. A cult grew up which followed his teachings, but it was savagely suppressed. It wouldn't be the first time a new Christian holy place was located on the site of an old heresy. No Spaniard,' he continued, 'ever went on a Crusade. We had our own adventures here in Spain. It was the Camino, the Way of St James which saved Spain from becoming an Arab country for ever. Without it, the border of Europe would have been the Pyrenees.'

It was this new friend who first pointed out to me that Spain was dominated by Islam for longer than it has since been Christian. He also told me that there are more Jews in Spain than in Israel. In Hebrew Sephardim means people of Spain, and they were the people who, having originally settled in Spain before the Inquisition, then spread to England and the Americas. Although he had been on the pilgrimage himself several times, he had little time for the Church, pointing out that until 1834 two-thirds of the land in Galicia was owned by the monasteries, which were disgustingly rich. Much of the rest was owned by absentee landlords who were deeply unpopular. 'You will find here that the people are suspicious and frightened of those who ride on horses. It reminds them too much of the oppression of the past.' He was also dismissive of the monarchy, saying that the Bourbons had never done anything for Spain. I suggested that the filth and litter of the Spanish countryside was a national disgrace and that it would be a good cause for the King to take up as it would, in my opinion, do more for his country's image and tourism than anything else. He agreed that this might be a good idea and could certainly do no harm. Having resolved his country's problems on this amicable note we staggered up to bed.

DAY 21 Tuesday 29th August   CEBREIRO TO SAMOS

'I have seen dawn and sunset on moors and windy hills
Coming in solemn beauty like slow old tunes of Spain.'
                                             John Masefield

We awoke to the sound of ravens passing overhead, their unmistakable deep croaks reminding me of home as they travel to their daytime feeding grounds high on the moors. At dawn the misty mountain ranges of Galicia stretched like Chinese silk screens on silver-lined clouds to the far horizon. Each ridge was etched on the haze rising from the valley behind it.

The English ladies were emerging from their tent as, after feeding and watering the horses, I trimmed some loose skin off their hooves where they had cut themselves on the sharp stones of yesterday's lanes. I was using a rather fearsome-looking curved knife, which I waved at them – meaning to be friendly – as they hurried past to the washroom. Not liking the look of Duque's sore, which had held up well recently but was today a little tender, I prepared to dress it with mercurichrome. He twitched just as I was holding the open bottle over his back and the entire contents was splashed on to the front of my jeans. I was really annoyed at ruining a perfectly good pair of trousers, but when I came into the dining room looking as though I had castrated myself the ladies gave a little whimper and scurried out. It was impossible to explain!

Too late to ask them intelligent questions now, we paused beside the *pallozas* as we rode out of Cebreiro. Solidly built circular dry-stone granite walls supported heavy thatched roofs. The stone lintels were massive and they had no chimneys. At least they must have been warm in winter, if unpleasantly dark and smoky inside. They are valuable in that they exemplify how our ancestors must have lived for thousands of prehistoric years. Probably the hut circles on the Cornish moors are the remains of very similar structures; on the edge of my own land are the remains of a group of about eighty such dwellings dating from the Bronze Age. The huts were between 5 and 10 metres in diameter, so quite as big as those at Cebreiro when standing. They would have formed a substantial settlement with a population of several hundred and life could have been quite exciting. The Bronze Age was the time when specialization began, when the wheel was invented and when people began to trade and travel by horse. Dazzled by the high speed of modern travel, it is easy to forget that for thousands of years vast distances were covered by much slower means. We know that for at least a thousand years pilgrims have been walking between Britain and Galicia, and we may assume that they have done so from the dawn of time. Even so, I found it strange to think that the wild inhabitants of prehistoric Bodmin Moor might have visited similar Celtic peoples in Galicia and stayed in houses identical to those at home.

The succession of little villages, huddled around their diminutive churches in the folds of the mountain through which we rode that day, had much the same feel to them, although their roofs were made of slate instead of thatch; often crudely cut thick slabs of it. The contrast to the rest of Spain was dramatic. This was Celtic cosiness, designed to keep out the mist and rain of the highlands. Greenery of trees and grass everywhere in the valleys, purple heather and dark broom on the hillsides. Old ladies in black sat peeling onions or doing nothing; few glanced up as we passed. Our friend had been right; here we would have to go out of our way to break the ice. Even the dogs ignored us. Some barked dutifully when they saw us or heard the clatter of the horses from the yards or gardens where they were confined, but none showed signs of the savagery other pilgrims have reported as one of the major hazards on the Way. The only ferocious ones we met were those chained up in towns, bored to insanity by their confined lives and driven to wild hysteria by our passing. Loose dogs were often quite friendly.

The only alien note introduced into the perfect bucolic charm of the countryside through which we were passing was struck by the terrible electricity pylons which marched relentlessly through valleys and over ridges. Once I counted four different systems running side by side, ranging down from the great 'Eiffel Towers' of a major grid system to the wooden poles leading from a local transformer. Without them the view would have been perfect; with them it was hideous, even though the narrow stony Way wound below them between hedges of juniper and wild flowers. We wished that they could have been sited so as to intrude less on the landscape. This was cattle country still, where large beige cows grazed the good grass; there were fewer cultivated fields. Some vegetable patches and orchards lay near the villages and one of these was guarded by a strange scarecrow. A caricature face had been painted on a white mask, with red cheeks and lips beneath a sailor's peaked cap. A gun-like stick was attached to one extended arm which pointed in the air, string from the end being tied to the other arm. When the wind blew it would move and look like someone shooting at seed- and fruit-stealing birds.

Louella noticed that her horse was favouring one of his front feet, and when we dismounted to see if there was a stone lodged in it we found that he had cast the shoe. Since we had not heard it fall and so did not know how far back along the path it might be, we decided not to look for it but instead to fit the hard rubber overshoe which we carried against just such an emergency. It looked clumsy and unlikely to stay on, but the clever method of attaching it with side clips worked well and Guadalquivir walked on contentedly.

We paused at the village of Triacastela to rest in the sun in front of the church tower, which has three stone castles carved below the belfry. Today it is another sleepy place which was once a bustling entrepôt, benefiting from the traffic of pilgrims through its deep, fertile valley. Perhaps in recognition of this, one of the family tombs in the graveyard was decorated lavishly with real scallop-shells stuck on the plaster in patterns and forming a large cross in the centre.

The meadows beside the Río Ouribio were subdivided into narrow paddocks, like those around Herrerias back in León on the other side of the mountain. However, instead of being fenced with wooden stakes, now upright slate slabs were used – stockproof and exactly similar to those of north Cornwall. It felt good to see something so familiarly Celtic. Fruitful farms between wooded gorges led us to a bend in the road from which we could look down on the rooftops of the great ancient monastery of San Julián de Samos. We had been looking forward to staying in a monastery and this huge rambling place with courtyards and gardens tucked away between a network of grey roofs and towers looked promising. Surely there would be a corner for our horses to graze and for us to camp beside them? Sited on much older foundations, in the 16th century it had been rebuilt to accommodate several hundred Benedictine monks, who would allow pilgrims to share their food for three days before they asked them to move on. It also used to house one of the great libraries of Spain, but in 1837 a law was passed giving the state responsibility for the upkeep of church property and as a result much was disposed of. Sacks of priceless books were sold to the local peasants, presumably as fuel. Our friend in Cebreiro had told us that after the Second World War, when petrol was virtually unobtainable in Spain, the abbot of Samos had cornered the supply and stored large quantities in the cellars – selling it on the black market to support his uneconomic establishment with its dwindling population of monks. Unfortunately in 1951 it caught fire, causing the biggest explosion ever heard in Galicia and destroying the rest of the library. Undeterred, the abbot had gone on a fund-raising tour in America and raised enough money to completely rebuild the destroyed parts of the monastery. Today the echoing cloisters are populated by fewer than a dozen monks. As we rode up to the walls discussing what we had been told, we were amazed to see two echoes of the past being re-enacted as though to remind us of Samos's recent history.

From a high window two old monks were throwing down bundles of books or magazines tied up with string, which were landing with loud thumps on the pavement below. We wondered what they might be, but resisted the temptation to ride over and look. Some remaining heretical texts from the vanished library? Copies of *Playboy*? We will never know. Next to the growing pile of paper was an old-fashioned petrol pump where another monk was filling up a car. It seemed as if some things never changed at Samos.

After this auspicious start, our reception at the main gate was a disappointment. The unfriendly monk on duty simply said 'No' both to the horses and to us. If we chose to return at 8.00 without them there might be accommodation for us, but nothing I said could persuade him that there was any space to graze or camp. Disconsolately we rode on, cheated for once of what had promised to be a memorable night. The Mayor of Samos was drinking outside his own café in the square, and in no time at all he had fixed us up with an excellent field close to a farmhouse a couple of kilometres beyond the village. He even produced an elderly gentleman who had been an army blacksmith during the war; on being demobilized, he told me as we worked together on Guadalquivir's new shoe, he had become a very successful butcher and was now retired. He had not put on a shoe for forty years, but did an excellent job. When I begged him to accept payment he declined graciously, saying that life had been good to him and he would be happy to oblige us again should we be passing that way.

We dined in the Mayor's back room on an excellent paella, the *especialidad de la casa*. Through the open door on to a terrace we could see the bulk of the monastery with more than a hundred dark windows overlooking walled gardens. Only one was lit. Framed in it was a cowled figure reading at a desk.

That night it rained for the first time since we had left the foothills of the Pyrenees. We had crossed the hot plains of Castile and León without a drop, but now we were well and truly in Galicia. George Borrow writes that the Gallegans call their drizzling mists '*bretima*' and that 'there is never any lack of them in their country'.

DAY 22 Wednesday 30th August   SAMOS TO PORTOMARÍN

*L*oud cockerels woke us at 5.00 am and we were up and saddled as the first rays of the sun began to dry our tents. Under the dripping trees of a thickly wooded valley we rode on to Sarria. Leading the horses on foot up steep cobbled alleys, we passed through the old medieval part of the town and up to the ruined castle. Here we stopped and rested by a slim granite cross on which Christ, the Virgin and two small supporters gazed out over the smoky haze of the modern town below. Nearby was the convent of the Magdalen now run as a school by the Fathers of Mercy, where we had our 'passports' stamped. Inside was a pleasant Gothic cloister full of flowers, but we were not encouraged to linger as priests and builders bustled about erecting scaffolding for some urgent repairs. In any case we were anxious to get out of town and back into the good Galician countryside ahead.

A steep descent to the Río Celeiro, which we crossed by a narrow old stone bridge, brought us to some of the best pilgrim travel yet. Deep, partly overgrown leafy lanes, redolent of the hordes which had passed through them on their way to Santiago, wound through ancient chestnut and oak woods. Away from roads or the sound of traffic, secret little green tracks led from one tiny village to another, each with its own small church. Sometimes the Way was stony and we dawdled, picking fat blackberries and an occasional apple, plum or fig. At other times there was grass or hard earth when we could give the horses their heads and fly along, ducking below overhanging branches and careering around blind corners or skidding to a stop if there was an obstruction.

The only people we saw were farmers working in their fields, raking hay or resting in the shade. Often the whole family would be sitting silently together, perhaps four generations, the children as still as their parents and grandparents, just staring into space. Perhaps the work was so strenuous that they needed every moment of rest to husband their resources, but there was something strange about the way they ignored us and seemed frozen in time. We knew that if we stopped and made friends they would inevitably be kind and communicative in due course; but simply seeing us ride by, would they comment after we were out of sight or just pretend we had not happened? The same thoughts had troubled us in China where we had been a far more unexpected sight in the remote countryside yet where, in contrast to the overpowering reception in towns and villages, country people seemed to be pretending that we did not exist. The answer is that we should travel much more slowly, having the courtesy to give each person met en route conversation and news, and receiving hospitality in return. Although we were a thousand times nearer this ideal than those flashing past in their cars on the main road some miles away, and although we could afford to stop and chat more often than those on foot desperately chalking up the miles before nightfall, we still sometimes regretted the change of pace today which prevents us from ignoring time. On the whole our lives are longer than those of our ancestors, yet we seem to have less time than them and to be always in a hurry.

The church of Santiago de Barbadelo was a lovely surprise. Once it was attached to a monastery founded in A.D. 874. Now only a ruined country house remains on the site, which used to be an important staging post for pilgrims on the Way. The church itself was locked, as sadly we found to be the case all too often in Spain, but it was the Romanesque doorways which we would have been sorry to miss. Both were tremendously satisfying in their simple perfection, the blocks of stone forming their vaulting so uncompromising in their flawless fit that looking at them it was impossible, for the moment, to imagine any other sort of arch. On the tympanum of the west door there was a crude figure of Christ with outstretched arms. Below, forming the lintel, a block of Celtic carving with nothing Christian about it: interlocking circles on either side of a curiously catlike design in the centre, supported on capitals depicting mythical beasts. Whoever built the church must have used old relics of previous monuments on the site, but he blended them together so well that the resulting portal is pure enchantment. Or so it seemed to us on that magical summer morning when the granite glowed a pale apricot in the sunshine and an old crone in black with a single yellow tooth sat on the church wall and cackled at us.

An hour or two through woods and farms brought us to a bar where we stopped for a drink. It was also a village store, the shelves piled with all the necessities of rural life. Usually we did not bother to eat during the day, carrying only some raisins or a packet of biscuits, but suddenly we felt very hungry – happiness can cause hunger sometimes, I find, just as misery can create a craving for chocolate – and we scanned the shelves for something edible. Sardines! We bought a large tin each, the shopkeeper produced a loaf of fresh bread and we sated ourselves messily but very satisfactorily outside, sitting on the grass beside the horses.

A succession of tiny villages followed, the Way running through the muddy medieval central lane of each. Everything was solid and unsophisticated, the great slabs of slate matched by ponderous planks and granite gateposts sunk into the cottages' walls. This was now the country of *horreos*, surprisingly elegant raised storehouses which seem to be a *sine qua non* of every household in Galicia with even the slightest agricultural pretensions; and these were mostly built of granite, too, although we saw them made of wood and cement and even roofed with pantiles. Rectangular and sometimes surprisingly long – the Galician record is 30 metres at Carnota – the object must be to provide the greatest possible surface area for the drying cobs of maize which are stacked neatly in them after harvest. They stand on columns variously designed to keep the vermin out, usually the familiar 'mushrooms' of granite on which Cornish ricks used to be raised for the same purpose.

We noticed a few signs of efforts being made to drag this

supremely rustic region into the 20th century. Many of the wayside springs, where limpid water often gushed from the hillside to trickle over a mossy bank between clumps of ferns and finally settle in a granite trough, bore recently placed symbols indicating whether the water was or was not potable. Some of the muddier lanes had been surfaced with concrete where they passed two or three houses; and many of these sported a new and hideous design of metal-framed windows. It was easy to regret these signs of progress and to wish that they had been left in their picturesque simplicity, but we had to admit that where there were pigsties on either side and cows passed daily on their way to be milked, the lanes must have been hideous quagmires when it rained. And doubtless the new windows were a great comfort, keeping out the howling draughts of winter; but why did they have to be so ugly?

It must have been a good summer in Galicia as well as in Cornwall, for the acorns were the largest we had ever seen, hanging almost like bunches of ripe grapes from the branches overhanging the lanes. Irresistible to grab handfuls as we passed, pop them easily out of their cups and lob them at each other. Louella and I are lucky in both being inexhaustible conversationalists, so that we tend to chatter inconsequentially as we ride along. This not only helps to pass the time, especially on the long stretches of open country which, on a horse, cannot be avoided; it also helps us to get to know each other better and better, to discuss our children and their futures, and to air any idea which drifts into our minds. Louella has an excellent memory for names and for recording incidents whether real or the plots of books or films. I have a more magpie mind, in which trivia seem to accumulate. Occasionally I can dredge up a suitable piece of doggerel which it gives me disproportionate pleasure to quote. As we rode through this enchanted landscape I managed to come up with:

> Don't view me with a critic's eye,
> But pass my imperfections by.
> Large streams from little fountains flow,
> Tall oaks from little acorns grow.

We saw our first prehistoric stone circle that day. It was big as a small football field in circumference, and that was exactly what it was being used for. The goal-posts were placed at either end and the standing stones formed the boundary.

At last we emerged on a ridge overlooking the valley of the Río Mino, Galicia's most important river which, rather as the Tamar does for Cornwall, rises not far from the north coast and flows south to cut off most of the region from the rest of the world, isolating it in the Atlantic. In 1962 the river was dammed at this point to create the large reservoir called the Embalse de Belesar. This flooded the ancient pilgrim town of Portomarín and the bridge built in 1120 by Pedro Peregrino, but the town was faithfully rebuilt higher up on the far bank, the stones of its churches being numbered and repositioned. As we looked across at them, the regular, box-like white houses spread out neatly on the hillside and reflected in the waters of the lake reminded us at first of Celesteville in the Babar books. However, once we had ridden over the new bridge which spans the reservoir at its central narrows, we found that the creation of a modern model town using old salvaged materials had worked very well indeed. Cobbled streets led between colonnaded pavements outside the shops, so that one could window-shop out of the rain. There was a delightfully colonial feel to the town, a faded elegance which was entirely unexpected but seemed to have imbued its citizens with strong civic pride. The policeman was the most friendly and helpful we had yet met, immediately showing us to the purpose-built market where there were covered alcoves in which we could set up camp, and a central paddock where he said the horses could safely graze on the rank grass and weeds under some trees.

The main church, which was originally built in the 13th century, has been described as one of the best works of Galician Romanesque art. The whole building had the solidity, strength and harmony we had come to recognize, and we were filled with admiration not only for the original builders but also for those who had repositioned it so well barely 25 years earlier so that it looked as though it had always stood there. Beasts abounded on the capitals, sinuous, strange and symbolic, and on the tympanum of the north door there was a charming Annunciation. The angel was rather stout, with curly hair, like a well-fed country parson. The Virgin looks appalled at the news he is bringing her, rejecting it with palms upraised. Between them is a surprisingly art nouveau fruit tree. The doorways were, as always, the most fascinating and satisfying features, combining their wonderful compatibility of arch and columns with delightful car-vings. This time it was the twenty-four Elders of the Apocalypse seated around Christ Pantocrator.

And round about the throne were four and twenty seats: and upon the seats I saw four and twenty elders sitting, clothed in white raiment; and they had on their heads crowns of gold . . . having everyone of them harps, and gold vials full of odours, which are the prayers of saints. And they sung a new song . . .*

The Old Men at Portomarín had no crowns and they were holding a whole variety of instruments in their hands which we strove to identify. A few verses later in Revelation there is an odd echo of

*Revelation, chapters 4, 5.

Santiago Matamoros where St John, his twin brother, writes. 'And I saw, and behold a white horse: and he that sat on him had a bow; and a crown was given unto him: and he went forth conquering, and to conquer.' The easiest instruments to recognize were an Irish harp and a lute, both unchanged today, but many were worn or obscure. We felt these representations of orchestras must be useful for the study of medieval music, since presumably they were carved from life; it was good to know that they would not have to play for eternity submerged.

Six months later, back in Cornwall, we were to hear the great expert on medieval music, Mary Remnant, give one of her lecture-recitals on the music of the Pilgrimage to Santiago. Playing a score of the strange instruments in turn, she brought alive so many of the scenes we had seen carved on churches. Courageously singing herself, encouraging members of the audience to have a go and charmingly involving the children by letting them hold and work the bells and tambourines, she recreated the atmosphere of medieval pilgrimage quite magically. We began to understand the important role which music must have played for all those weary travellers – both as recreation and fun en route and in the evenings as well as in church and monastery, when it accompanied the spiritual experiences being orchestrated by the clergy as the pilgrim was led towards the final climactic experience. Dimly remembered biblical names of instruments like the shawm, psaltery and rebec became familiar in her wonderfully deft hands. We wished we had had the experience before setting out, since we would have understood and appreciated so much more. Knowing of our recent pilgrimage, she called me up to blow a horn similar to Roland's Olifant. Anxious to please and impress, I put my all into blowing a great blast, as though summoning Charlemagne, but all that emerged was a faint and embarrassing squawk. As my eyes popped, cheeks bulged, face reddened, I looked helplessly towards Mary, who said quietly, 'Relax.' I did so and immediately the pure note came. I held it as long as I could, eyes closed and imagining myself back at Roncesvalles in the beech woods and crags of the high Pyrenees.

Just outside the town a parador was built in the hope that Portomarín would become a successful tourist resort, offering boating and fishing on the lake as well as the delights of the reconstructed buildings. This had clearly not come to pass and the paradox, as we named it, had been abandoned to be overgrown with creepers. Like Sleeping Beauty's castle, everything was still there but covered in dust and cobwebs. Merlin greatly enjoyed our explorations, since he could be lifted up to peer through the windows and to describe the bedrooms with their rotting furniture and the dining room still laid for a dinner that would now never be served.

DAY 23 Thursday 31st August   PORTOMARÍN TO PALAS DO REI

Leaving Portomarín, we crossed an arm of the reservoir by a high narrow bridge. Far below we could see the fields and foundations of part of the old town, now exposed to the air again as the water was so low following the long dry summer. For a time the stream, usually submerged below still water, was a stream again, and our shadows passed where once real animals grazed beside it and drank from it.

Now along tracks and country lanes, we passed more small villages where bullock carts, dung-heaps, vegetable gardens all gave a sense of hard work and rustic life. It was green, wooded, wet Celtic country, dank and sunless in the valleys, a chill wind blowing out on the exposed fields and hilltops. For the first time since leaving the Pyrenees we dug our sweaters out of our saddlebags and were glad of them. Stretches of open heather moorland lay between the valleys. As we crossed a country road running along a ridge, a car passed us, then stopped. A thoroughly shifty character, whom we recognized at once as a horse coper from the way he examined our mounts and stood in our path to do so, then asked us if we wanted to sell them. It would have been interesting to know if we could have recouped our money had we decided to buy and sell again as on previous rides, rather than hire them from Pablo, but we found the idea of even negotiating with him so distasteful that we assured him they were not for sale. Excusing ourselves on the grounds that we were in a hurry, we rode around him and away from the road. Although we had not grown nearly as fond of Duque and Guadalquivir as we had instantly become and remained on meeting Thibert and Tiki, our Camargues, we realized that we did not like the idea that they might go to a new owner at all, and moreover that when it was all over we would miss them.

Both in the villages we rode through and those we glimpsed occasionally in the countryside between, were some more solid and pleasing houses than the general run which were often little more than hovels. Again we were struck by the absence of any which had had care and money spent on them. Many could have been easily turned into attractive and comfortable desirable residences, the kind which in Britain and much of the rest of Europe now sell for highly inflated figures. It was not as though there were no signs of extravagance among the general poverty. Every now and then we would see, stuck out in a field without benefit of garden or shelter, a modern Dallas bungalow, complete with picture windows, crazy paving and pretentious colonnaded patio. Utterly lacking in character, they might have been bought from a mail order catalogue. These

One of the Pallozas preserved at
Cebreiro. These buildings, which
were lived in by locals until recently
and are still occupied by pilgrims, are
probably the same as the bronze age
dwellings whose traces are seen as
hut circles

Right: The Romanesque doorway at
Vilar de Donas

Below: The tomb of a 'Verray, Parfit Gentil Knight' of the order of St James of the Sword

Below left: A carving in the knights' cloister in Najera of a rider resting with his horse

Left: St James the gentle pilgrim

Bottom: Old house in Galicia

Top: Resting and writing up our diaries on Monxoi before riding into Santiago

Above: Riding joyfully out of the Plaza de Obradoiro after arriving safely at the end of our pilgrimage

Finisterre, the end of the known world until 1492

were the houses of the returning 'Americanos', Galicians who had emigrated – which a great many do – made a fortune, the destiny of rather fewer, and then returned to live in their homeland. When we saw the first of those meretricious and incongruous houses we looked at each other in amazement, then said simultaneously, 'Where have I seen one of these before?' It only took a moment to work it out. The Irish who have come back to the Old Sod favour a similar style of building and they too seem to reject the fine architecture with which their land is graced. Perhaps both peoples are unconsciously rejecting the works of their past oppressors; or perhaps returning emigrants simply tend to have bad taste.

Like many places along the Way, Palas do Rei has a long and distinguished history. Once the capital of the last Visigoth king, Witiza, at the start of the 8th century and favoured by subsequent medieval monarchs, it is now described as having 'no features of special interest' and most travellers hurry through. Those that stop all seem to report – as did Joan and Merlin when we met them outside the town – that the inhabitants were unusually unhelpful and dismissive of the needs of pilgrims. Having set up a camp in a field next to the town football ground, we drove to see the church at Vilar de Doñas, 10 kilometres off our route, which several people had told us was a place not to be missed. They were right. It was another breathtaking experience, enhanced once more by the simplicity and genuine poverty of its setting.

The Doñas were two Galician noblewomen who paid to have the church and a now vanished monastery built. The weight of the solid slate roof and the heavy granite blocks from which the church is made seems to have dragged it down, so that it sits low in the ground and is very damp inside, but it is full of delights. The Romanesque doorway, which is concealed by a sort of half cloister, consists of five concentric arches, each composed of different designs and leading naturally to three elegant columns. Beside it grew a tall fig tree and the old woman, whom we had come to expect at these otherwise silent and abandoned places, gathered some and gave them to us. They were almost black with ripeness and musty like sherry trifles inside.

She urged us to enter and we found ourselves surrounded by the lovely tombs of the Knights of the Military Order of St James of the Sword, to whom the church was given in the 12th century soon after the Order was founded in 1175. Just as the Knights Templar were bound to protect pilgrims going to the Holy Land, so it has long been believed that it was the duty of these knights to drive the Moors from Spain and to guard pilgrims as they trudged towards the shrine of the saint from the highwaymen and bandits who beset the Way. But, as Professor Derek Lomax of Birmingham University, the expert on the Order, has demonstrated, they were far too busy driving the Moors from Spain to do any such thing. However, St James symbolized the Reconquest of Spain and these warrior knights represented the bloodthirsty side of his image. Their motto was, 'The sword is red with the blood of Arabs' (*Rubet ensis sanguine Arabum*). To qualify for membership of the Order they had to be chaste, uncircumcized (so as to prove they were not Moors or Jews), and to accept the doctrine of the Virgin Birth.

Far from looking warlike, the figures on the tombs had charming faces, 'verray, parfit gentil knights' we felt. There was green moss on the walls and floor which felt wet to the touch, even on a hot, dry day at the end of August. In winter water must run down the walls. The tombs seemed unaffected, but the astonishing 14th-century paintings in the central apse were suffering badly, the paint and plaster peeling off before our eyes. Christ the Saviour directly behind the altar was the best preserved figure; sketched more than painted, he looked a gentle, sensitive soul, suffering mental as well as physical anguish from his bleeding wounds. A delicate person with strange, twisted lips, I have never seen another Christ quite like it. The figures around which had survived were different too, more like Greek gods than Christian ones. It was tragic to see such rare and beautiful paintings deteriorating so fast. The door of the church was open wide, presumably to let in the air and keep the mildew down, but this did not seem to be doing much good and each damp winter would do more damage. There was ample evidence that the church was regularly used; there were new pews made of pale pine in the body of the church, books, kneelers, candles, flowers and a robed Virgin, but no priest. We spent an hour alternating between joy at each new discovery and horror at its soaking setting. There were more paintings around the walls from different periods, including one said to represent the two original donors, and lots of fascinating carvings and tombstones. On the main altar was a touching granite retable depicting the descent from the cross. The gentle faces of the weeping Marys and a bearded figure, perhaps Joseph of Arimathaea, cradling Christ's head, are simple and moving. They, too, were covered in green slime mould.

Led by the old lady, we went in search of the priest. His house, which was attached to the church, had almost completely collapsed – the pantile roof falling in, the windows sightless without their frames. Around the front, behind an untrimmed vine, we found the front door and through the window beside it could see into an almost bare room with a pile of books and a picture of the Pope. It was incomprehensible to us that somewhere as precious as Vilar de Doñas, classified as a National Monument, should be so neglected and that the priest should be so very poor.

A short way from the church, in a grove of ancient oaks on a hill, was another building which our old lady described as the Hermitage. It is not mentioned in any of the guides, but we now saw what could easily happen if the neglect was allowed to continue. An attractive but much later building with a Renaissance portal and pantile roof, it had passed the point of no return; the roof had collapsed, the altar screen was rotting and grass grew in the nave. It would be only a matter of time now before it either fell down or was taken over by a farmer as a cowshed.

On the way back to our camp, we saw an old-fashioned wash-house where spring water flowed into two large stone tanks surrounded by ribbed ledges for beating the clothes on. We took all our dirty washing there and spent a happy hour scrubbing and rinsing in the cold water.

'What a splendid system,' I enthused. 'Really impossible to improve on.' Carried away by the picturesque scene, I stopped working to stand back and admire the sight of Louella and Joan up to their elbows in cold suds and slapping their smalls on the stone slab.

'This is much better than the hot water in the bath in the parador at León, where you last did a big wash, isn't it?' I gushed. They seemed unconvinced.

DAY 24 Friday 1st September   **PALAS DO REI TO ARZÚA**

When travelling with horses, disaster is always just around the corner. It was a windy night and they both escaped, dragging their pickets but luckily not wandering as far as a road where, trailing ropes behind them, they might have caused a horrifying accident. While we were tacking them up, Guadalquivir stepped on Merlin's foot as he tried to help. Once again everything went into slow motion . . . the agonized yell, the continuing pressure as more and more weight seemed to be applied and his tiny foot sank into the fortunately soft earth of the field beneath the large hoof. The lifting, comforting and examining for broken bones, blood or bruising. None, happily, but there so easily might have been. . . .

We had not been riding for half an hour when Duque decided to go lame on his off fore-foot. There are so many things which can go wrong with a horse's foot that one must always take lameness seriously, and I stopped several times to feel and poke and prod but without finding anything amiss. Stones are easily lodged next to the frog, small cuts can become infected, bones and tendons can become sore from knocks and twists, especially on the kind of rough stony ground we had been covering for the last few days. There is an old saying, 'No foot, no horse', and we were determined not to have to give up when so near our destination. In the end I decided he was faking and it seemed that I was right as, after a few more attempts to gain sympathy and attention by limping for several yards, he gave it up and went on well.

Gentle rolling wooded country now, with a succession of pleasant villages and a well-marked Way to follow. For some time there had been regular stone markers at least every kilometre and sometimes every hundred metres, indicating how much further there was to go. Inevitably the number of people undertaking each stage of the pilgrimage would increase as the final stretch into Santiago itself approached. Although by now we had left all the walking pilgrims we had met along the Way far behind, we had not seen any new ones for some time. Looking down from the lovely Gothic bridge at Furelos, we now saw a young Spanish couple washing their feet in the mill-race, their staffs and pilgrim guide instantly revealing them for what they were. We waved and exchanged greetings, but the camaraderie of our earlier meetings had evaporated, perhaps because each couple suspected that the others were not completing a proper pilgrimage as they were themselves. Nevertheless they made a delightful picture as they sat facing half a dozen solid brown cows which had been driven down to the river to drink. So did the old man leading two oxen attached to a cart which was almost entirely constructed of wood and in which, had there been horses in the shafts instead, Boadicea would not have looked out of place. Only the rims of the hefty wooden wheels were of iron, and lashed on to the cart was the long-shafted wooden plough to which the oxen would be attached on arrival at their field. We had seen these extremely practical ploughs being used before, but had not realized how very basic and ancient was their design. The wooden blade with its metal tip was simply attached to the shaft by a twisted length of creeper. Everything, including the yokes and handles, had quite clearly been crudely carved by the old man himself. We were back in country where the minimum was bought or traded and the maximum constructed out of local materials; these are the attributes of tribal societies which I have always most admired, giving as they do a freedom from dependence on external forces beyond their control. Doubtless, now Spain has entered the Common Market, the rate of change in agriculture will accelerate and such satisfying sights will become even rarer.

Melide was a busy little market town where we stopped outside the public library and took it in turns to visit the church of San Pedro. Once past the excellent 12th-century doorway, we found ourselves in an extraordinary world of vulgar Catholic kitsch, the very worst we had yet met. A wooden Christ lay tucked up in a coffin with real hair and bedclothes; a Virgin clutched at the dagger sticking out of her breast and oozed blood. Other macabre treats awaited those so inclined, but neither of us was tempted to linger and we rode on out of town along the narrow ancient Calle Principal to the much simpler and prettier church of Santa María with its pleasing Romanesque apse. Close by there was a bar where we stopped for a drink. The owner greeted us effusively and amazed us by breaking into perfect English when we told him where we came from. It turned out that he had worked as a waiter at the Tudor Rose at Virginia Water, Surrey. Guessing our requirements without asking, he pressed two excellent and huge bacon-and-egg sandwiches on us.

Arzúa, which we reached by mid afternoon, is the last major town on the Way. Joan and Merlin had set up the tents in the garden of the owner of the Don Manuel Camp-site on the edge of town. We were a bit worried that the horses would damage their neat lawns, camellia bushes and flower-beds and so had to scurry about clearing up behind them and moving their pickets, but they behaved well and his family were very kind to us, insisting that it would be all right to leave them in their care.

We drove to the Cistercian monastery of Sobrado dos Monxes, originally founded in 1192 but completely rebuilt on a vast scale between the 16th and 18th centuries. A greater contrast with the little stone parish churches of the Galician villages we had been passing through for the last week would be hard to find. The façade was lofty, imposing, ornate, calculated to intimidate visitors and acolytes alike, though on close inspection grass could be seen sprouting from the twin towers. The monk who let us in wore the white habit with a brown scapular of his Order, whose first Abbot and founding father was an Englishman, St Stephen Harding. Perhaps for this reason he was exceptionally kind to us, letting us stay after closing time and wander wherever we wanted. Here, as in Vilar de Doñas, there were horrifying signs of damp, the green mould creeping far up the walls of the church and along the stone corridors and cloisters. But there any resemblance ended. This was a religious building on the grand scale and everything around us was massive, with soaring columns constantly drawing our eyes upwards. Even the medieval kitchen, which had survived the restoration, seemed to carry the same message, its colossal circular central chimney carrying the souls of the faithful as well as the smoke of their cooking up to heaven. All that was lacking was worshippers and music. Such monumental effort demanded action.

Religious fervour has produced so many of the greatest works of man. As I gazed up and half heard the echoes of past services, I wondered whether faith had been the inspiration through which so much talent had manifested itself or simply a convenient vehicle, perhaps the only one available to men of genius in their time. Mozart, whose music had formed such a constant background to our pilgrimage – being the muzak of our camps – appears not to have been a particularly religious person, yet he was expected to produce quantities of ecclesiastical music to order, and did so, even composing some of his earliest work in the Benedictine monastery at Lambach. The most uplifting church music of all, Allegri's *Miserere*, was what I associated with the great Gothic and Renaissance interiors of these wonderful churches. Heard only during Holy Week in the Sistine Chapel, for 200 years its score was a closely guarded secret and it must represent pure religiously inspired music if anything does. It was Mozart who gave it to the world, being able to write it down after listening to it only twice when he attended services in the Vatican in 1769. At the time it was composed, no one would have doubted that it was the result of divine inspiration, but was Mozart's theft divine intervention? Andrew Lloyd-Webber's *Benedictus* was the right music to go with the splendid Romanesque portals, we decided, with its stately roundness and sense of order; but listening to music is a very personal experience and people will always hear it in different ways. There appears to be a need for something to believe in, for music to be comprehensible and appeal to the emotions; once that belief is found then all kinds of inspiration can be channelled through it. Under industrial society, when spiritual values were rejected in favour of the nihilism of a 'modern' approach to everything, music – like much other artistic expression – tended to become abstruse and shallow. Will the passion for nature, all life and the rich diversity of our planet have the same power to inspire as the great religions of the past? Since the ancient civilizations of Egypt, Greece, Rome and indeed China worshipped many gods, there seems no reason why not and it will be interesting to see, as the green revolution develops, if artistic creation in all its fields keeps pace with it.

With its 800th anniversary coming up in 1992, our monastic friend told us that massive restoration work was about to be undertaken by the members of his community. Using high-pressure hoses, they would clean all the walls and transform the buildings to their former glory. Being Cistercians of the Common Observance, they would be able to talk as they worked, unlike those of the Strict Observance who are otherwise known as Trappists. 'You never know,' he said wistfully, 'such a great undertaking might even bring us some novices.'

*L*ooking at Louella as we set off on our last full day's riding, I thought again how remarkably tough and resilient she was. While I pretended to her and others that her fortitude was merely her way of showing that she could do anything I could do better, I knew that there was much more to it than that. This had been quite a tough journey, in spite of our excellent and reliable back-up. The burning sun of the Spanish plains sears the skin, yet she had seemed oblivious to it. Both of us were by now burnt a dark brown, but while my skin was scorched like an old apple hers was still as fresh as when she left England. Her hair was much blonder than its natural auburn, but still it looked healthy and full. There had been no visits to hairdressers or beauty salons along the Way, just regular washing in usually cold water with ordinary soap. No smells of stale scent or tired lotions, just a perfect advertisement for natural healthy living; and yet she seemed unaware of it. Utterly lacking in self-pity, she ignored the discomforts and problems of the journey, refusing to allow them to interfere with her enjoyment. Since most physical distress originates in the mind, she proved daily that there is no need to be uncomfortable if you are happy. This is something I knew well in theory, but I needed her example to stop me from seeking sympathy for the aches and pains of long hours in the saddle, and she never let me down.

That day we rode through sylvan glades and tranquil countryside which must have seen the passing of countless eager pilgrims hurrying along the last stretch of their journeys from all over Europe. It should have felt different, knowing and welcoming in a special way. We expected the people living there to indicate somehow that they knew how excited we were, not by lining the streets and cheering but perhaps by giving us a special smile or wave. Such, however, is not the Galician way and there was nothing save the now rapidly reducing numbers on the milestones to show how near we were to the end.

There even seemed to be fewer churches along the Way, and none of great interest, while the villages were more prosperous with the beginnings of a suburban feel to them at times. Between them ran the narrow Way, often only a path between tall hedges but always worn by the mark of countless feet. At each farm there was a *horreo*, mostly empty at this season, waiting for the corn to be harvested. One actually straddled the Way between two walls and we rode under it. Some of the woods were of old oak and pine where we could race the horses, risking everything, then stop and gather blackberries. Later they were of eucalyptus and we saw the devastation caused by fires. We knew that there had already been over 700 forest fires that year in Galicia, and we had seen three the day before not far from our route, casting black clouds into the sky and crackling ominously in the distance. The eucalyptus was brought to Spain some years ago by an Australian bishop. Now many people regard it as a pest, an ecological disaster which swamps other species and suppresses diversity, while being extremely prone to catching fire, from which it — but little else — usually recovers. The fires that year had been especially bad because of the drought, but many were started deliberately either for fun or by those who resented the trees on political grounds and because they deprived the people of land for agriculture.

Franco — who was born in Galicia, his father being a paymaster at the naval base of El Ferrol near Corunna — always kept a family house near there which he used to visit regularly. In his efforts to build up more timber resources he imposed on Galicia many compulsory plantations enclosing common land, mostly of pine, and the existence of these forests is still widely resented. This may be why so many of them catch fire.

The eucalyptus are still being planted, since they are so quick-growing that they are regarded as commercially viable. We found another reason to dislike them, apart from the environmental aspect. Since their barks peel, the yellow arrows painted on them to indicate which of the many tracks through the woods we should follow had often vanished with the bark, and we were lost several times.

For the first time now we began to hear aircraft passing high overhead. No regular flight paths had crossed the Way since we had begun, and the distant sound was unfamiliar. The civil airport, by which many pilgrims come to Santiago, lay between us and the city, and there was also an air force base not far away. The sky was clear blue and there were vapour trails visible through the trees. At mid-day, as we climbed a ridge hoping to have a good view ahead from the open top, we looked up and there in the heavens above us was a perfect cross, wide and fluffy, stretching from one side of the sky to the other to link all four corners of the world directly over our destination. Perhaps it was done deliberately by two jet pilots as a practical joke, perhaps it happens all the time; but I could not recall ever seeing vapour trails forming a complete right-angle cross in the sky before. As we watched, the straight clouds drifted apart and blurred into a haze. There was a high wind up there and no patterns stayed the same for long.

That wind was to hit us when at last, after skirting the boundary fence of the civil airfield, across the main runway of which the Way used to lead, after crossing the stream at Lavacolla where pilgrims used to wash before entering the city, we climbed Monxoi, the

Monte del Gozo, the ultimate *montjoie* from which the first sight of the city and its cathedral is gained. The mount of joy did not look at all as we had expected, imagining a grassy hill-top up which those millions of joyous pilgrims who had preceded us ran to fall exhausted and triumphant on the green turf beside a simple cairn of stones. The Pope had been there two weeks before – and so had half a million young pilgrims, swelling beyond all recognition the ranks of those who had walked and ridden horses or bicycles to meet him. This mound was where he had addressed them, and no one had attempted to clear it up following the great event. A vast wasteland of bare, trampled red earth stretched in all directions. Across it blew streamers of paper and plastic bags, while tin cans and bottles rolled along below. The sense of excitement the occasion had engendered lingered on. There were signs saying 'Heliporto' and 'Prohibido' protecting nothing now. There were people, heads bowed against the wind, picking their way to the spot where His Holiness had stood. Perhaps they were seeking to gain virtue from the papal sanctity given to the place, but they were more like the survivors of a nuclear holocaust picking over a municipal rubbish tip. The dust blown up by the wind obscured the view and far away below Santiago seemed like a mirage.

Below the summit, just beyond the little village of San Marcos, was a tiny hermitage set in a grove of oak trees. Whitewashed, windowless and locked, it was the Capilla of San Marcos, and Joan had set up our final camp-site there in the shelter of a low wall. The wind was not only strong, it was cold, and once we had tethered and fed the horses we were glad to escape from it and the dust it carried.

Late that night, the wind dropped for a while and we went to comfort the horses, who did not much like where they were but were happy enough with the hay we gave them, until it blew away again. Now the lights of the city could be seen clearly, the three spires of the Cathedral standing out against them. Far above, as though to emphasize the point we might have missed in the daylight with the vapour trails, there glowed a single star.

DAY 26 Sunday 3rd September   **SANTIAGO DE COMPOSTELA**

Guadalquivir escaped in the night and we were woken by his footsteps as he tramped about between the tents and knocked over the pots and pans of our kitchen. It was quite cold in the early dawn as we recaptured him and the wind blew the red dust around us and howled mournfully in the trees. As we prepared the horses for their entry to the city, the truck which was to take them back to Estella arrived – hours early – and we begged them to be patient while we completed this, the most important moment of our whole journey. They quite understood and went off to have a good breakfast.

Only five kilometres now lay between us and the saint. At first it was impossible to avoid the main road and there was a surprising amount of fast traffic for an early Sunday morning. Then we were in the cobbled back streets of Santiago de Compostela itself which were only just beginning to become awake and were still largely deserted. Sweet old ladies in black sat in their doorways and wished us God speed, family groups heading for Mass smiled at us and called, 'Hola, peregrinos', a few even clapped. We felt half-way between anti-climax and urgency.

In the last square, the Plaza de Cervantes, we stopped to water the horses and rest them for a moment. The sun was just catching the spires of the Cathedral ahead of us, church bells were ringing all over the town and the moment seemed just right as we mounted and rode the last few hundred metres. The descent was steeper than we had expected and the horses' shoes, now smooth and worn again, slipped dangerously on the cobbles. A sheer flight of steps led down in front of us, impassable for horses, and we had to detour to the right down a sloping roadway which led us into the Rúa de San Francisco under the high walls of the Reyes Catolicos Hotel. From this dark alley we rode out into the light and space of somewhere which can fairly dispute with the Piazza San Marco for the title of the finest public square in Europe: the Plaza del Obradoiro. A prosaic name (meaning workshop) for a place so beautiful, it comes from the main doorway at the top of the quadruple stone staircase, where for ten years workmen carved the blocks of golden Galician granite into Baroque fantasies and fitted them together to make the great façade which dominates the square. Hidden behind it lies the Pórtico de la Gloria, the 12th-century masterpiece of Mateo, the first but not the final destination of all pilgrims. The ultimate objective, the casket containing the supposed relics of the Saint himself, lies nearly a hundred metres away below the high altar.

Merlin came running across the empty square to greet us, as excited as we were at our arrival and looking very smart in his black Stubbie shorts and a clean white pilgrim shirt covered in scallops. We too had dressed properly for the occasion and, in addition to our usual riding gear with pilgrim decorations, had real pink scallop-shells around our necks. These had been given to me three months before when I was on my recce by Señor Ballesteros, the Director of Santiago's Tourist Office, and it felt good to be returning them to their city unbroken.

A group of tourists emerging from the Cathedral stared at us in amazement and delight for a moment before beginning to click away furiously at this sudden manifestation of real pilgrims riding up to the base of the steps on a pair of white horses. Guadalquivir and Duque seemed to realize it was an important occasion and stepped out proudly for once. We dismounted and tied them to the railings.

At that moment a whistle was loudly blown and one of the municipal guards in a peaked cap, who harry anyone rash enough to drive into the square, began to run towards us. Fortunately he was on the far side and so I had time to tell Louella to watch the horses and Merlin while I raced up the steps and through the door-way to thrust my fingers into the crevices of the central pillar, the Tree of Jesse, worn smooth by the touch of countless hands – the gesture which confirmed that I had arrived safely. With no time to linger then, I hurried down again to face the wrath of the guard.

'You and your horses are not allowed here,' the guard shouted furiously at me.

'Why don't you go on up and touch the Tree, darling?' I said in English to Louella, cold with anger at being harassed by petty bureaucracy at such a special moment. Then, in Spanish, to the guard, 'We are pilgrims. Is not the whole reason for the existence of Santiago to be a pilgrim city?'

'That may be so,' he answered crossly, 'but horses must stay outside at the cattle yards.'

'What nonsense!' I retorted. 'Even if there was such a law, which I doubt, we have ridden through every city between here and France and no one has ever stopped us. We are the first true horse pilgrims this year and you should welcome us. Look at the pleasure we are giving these tourists!'

'You must go now,' he shouted and began to talk ominously into his walkie-talkie, apparently summoning reinforcements. As we remounted he circled around us like an angry vulture. Ignoring him, we stood still for a few moments in front of the Cathedral. We would return later to see it all on foot, but now we simply wanted to show Duque and Guadalquivir our gratitude to them for having carried us all the way so resolutely, and to try to share with them the sense of achievement it gave us. Already lean when we had set out from Roncesvalles, they were no thinner now; they had no wounds or scars to show for the journey; even Duque's saddle-sore had miraculously healed itself in the last few days and almost returned to its original state when he had first arrived. They had done well and we thanked them.

Back at our camp we kissed them goodbye quickly and loaded

them into the truck for their nine-hour drive back to Estella, waving as they disappeared down the hill towards the main road. Then we hurried back into town to see the sights properly.

Like Venice, but only half the size, Santiago de Compostela has an infinity of enchantments to offer the dedicated tourist. It is a town which has been very little spoiled by modernity, and there are winding colonnaded streets where those who need to buy souvenirs to remind them where they have been are amply and professionally catered for by the local inhabitants. After all, they have been living off the pilgrim tourist industry for over a thousand years. It is also a University town, and colour is added to the bustling alleys by students in their harlequin gowns.

The Cathedral, containing as it does the object of veneration which brought every pilgrim there over the centuries, dominates Santiago in a way that St Mark's does not attempt to do. The Italian city's charms are spread out among the sunlight and water, which reflect her palaces and churches in a harmony which is beyond compare. The Galician holy city suffers so much rain that it has been called the chamber-pot of Spain. Although its granite walls and red pantile roofs thrive on all this moisture and scintillate when the sun does shine, sprouting flowering weeds and tufts of grass from every crack so that it seems sometimes as though it is a lost city abandoned to nature, yet the visitor is constantly drawn towards the physical and spiritual shelter of the great monument in its centre.

There are squares on all four sides of the Cathedral and space all around, so that the visitor can stand back to admire it. The greatest of all Romanesque pilgrimage cathedrals is largely hidden behind the Baroque features which were added in the 18th century when the building was finally completed. This style is often called Churri-gueresque after José Churriguera, the Spanish Michelangelo who was credited with creating it. A painter, sculptor and architect, he died in 1725, a dozen years before the Galician architect Fernando Casas y Novoa began to build the Obradoiro façade over the Pórtico de la Gloria. The Romanesque features which can still be seen – especially the wonderful Platerias Doorway in the southern transept – are rather swamped by all this Baroque, but there is no doubt that it is the greatest possible fun, a joyous outburst of reaction against the staid classicism of the early Renaissance. Every stone that can be carved is worked into a profusion of curves and patterns. Every available space reveals another statue of a saint or angel; the towers and cupolas scramble over each other to reach for the sky in a series of contortions which look, though half-closed eyes, almost like the craggy rocks of a romantic landscape or, again, the ruins of a long vanished civilization thrusting up out of the jungle. To add to this effect there was an orange lichen which crept across the stonework, giving it at times a tropical glow. St James and scallop-shells repeated everywhere remind one over and again what is the real purpose of the building.

Inside there can be no mistake, as we found from the moment we stood in front of the Pórtico de la Gloria, now with time to look at it. Originally the 200 carved figures were painted in bright colours and traces of paint remain on many, giving cheeks a pink glow and highlighting the edges of robes. There is so much action here, conversation pieces between prophets, saints and the apostles, who hold their symbols in their hands. St Luke even has his bull stretched across his knees like a lap-dog and is calmly writing his gospel on its back. Here in one place is the culmination of 12th–century carving, the result of twenty years' work by Master Mateo. On the back of the central column, with its Tree of Jesse which we had touched so briefly that morning, knelt the small carved figure of the master carver. According to tradition, those who touch their forehead against his will acquire some of his talent and his wisdom. Solemnly we did so.

Above the column sits St James, greeting each arrival with a benign smile and holding in his hands his staff and a scroll on which is written *Misit Me Dominus*, The Lord Sent Me.

Inside the body of the church we found ourselves captured, as pilgrims always must have been, by the gracefulness of the space around us, the perfection of Romanesque architecture at its apogee. It is through this space that, on special occasions, the giant *botafumeiro* – the largest incense censer in the world (made in 1602) – is swung to the eaves by eight men pulling on a rope. The purpose is to disperse the smoke of the fragrant burning gums and spices as widely as possible through the church, but the spectacle is one of pure theatre, an uplifting treat for the pilgrims, a heart-stopping and dangerous reminder of fear on childhood swings when the world turned upside down. Once, long ago, the *botafumeiro* is said to have continued its sickening swoop above the bowed heads of the congregation and flown out of a cathedral window; perhaps it will happen again.

We shuffled around with the crowd past the innumerable side chapels towards the high altar itself. Gilded, convoluted, lit from all sides, sparkling with silver and gold, festooned with angels and cherubs, it far surpassed any such Baroque excesses we had seen on the Way. Like a magnet it drew us to it until we mounted the steps inside and reached the ultimate figure of St James, the gilded silver statue which every pilgrim embraces as the final act of pilgrimage. Again we did what was expected and it felt good. Not in a great uplifting spiritual way – the ritual was too much of a tourist act for that – but with a deep sense of satisfaction at having completed what we had set out to do.

The Pilgrims' Office was set into the Cathedral facing on to the Plaza de la Quintana. We went round there, feeling a little self-conscious in front of the University students sitting in the sun on the wide flight of steps, and we presented the pilgrim 'passports' we had received at Roncesvalles, now full of stamps. Instead of immediately adding the Cathedral's own stamp in the spaces we had left at the end, the serious young clerk examined each 'passport' carefully, checking that the dates tallied with our story of having ridden all the Way. We had collected more than one stamp a day, and looking back through them already helped to remind us where we had been. Many were simple oblongs with a saint or coat of arms surrounded by the place name, but some stood out. Eunate showed the church surrounded by rays of sunlight and set in a scallop-shell; Santo Domingo de la Calzada had, predictably, the chickens in feathery profile; Chonina's bar had a jolly modern pilgrim with rucksack and staff; Cebreiro showed its chalice and Portomarín its bridge across the reservoir.

Satisfied, he wrote out Compostelas, rolled them up and presented them to us. It felt like receiving a school prize for a term's hard work.

The Hotel de los Reyes Católicos is the best known and perhaps the best of all the paradors in Spain. Staying there is commonly referred to as a unique experience, one in which I had indulged myself for one night on my recce. We had had our taste of such luxury in the equally beautiful Parador of San Marcos in León and, after collecting our letters from Reception, we strolled through the four superb Renaissance cloisters around and over which lie the guests' rooms. Everything is done with style and elegance; the furniture is antique, often massively carved from wood and for once not dwarfing its surroundings. The restaurant, where many of the exotic seafood specialities of Galicia are served, is vast with huge stone arches above very white starched linen napery, sparkling glassware and twinkling cutlery.

Instead of sampling the tiny green peppers of Padrón or the scallops in white wine, *vieras de Santiago*, we decided to exercise our right as pilgrims in possession of a Compostela to a free meal.

Starting in 1499, the hotel was built on the orders of Ferdinand of Aragon and Isabel of Castile, the Catholic monarchs after whom it is named and whose statues are included in the wonderful assemblage of carving around the main doorway. Not completed until 1678, it consists of a glorious riot of figures from Adam and Eve at

the bottom to St James himself and musical angels under the elegant
stone mouldings below the roof which run the whole length of the
main façade. It must be the grandest of all hotel entrances. The
purpose of all this sumptuous building was to minister to sick pilgrims, exhausted by their journey and in need of medical treatment
and rest. According to medieval records there were usually 200 or
more guests enjoying the facilities. Provided they did not overstay
their welcome nothing was too good for them and, being at the end
of the most popular pilgrimage in Christendom, it was regarded as
proof and justification of the faith which had drawn so many there.
Ferdinand and Isabel financed this hospital and many other pilgrim
facilities along the way from a tax on corn and wine which they
collected as a gesture of thanks to Santiago Matamoros, who had
brought about the *reconquista*, from those parts of Spain liberated
from the Moors. And thus Santiago became a rich city, able to build
extravagantly, encourage more pilgrims and so become richer still.

The tradition of giving free hospitality to pilgrims survived the
conversion of the hospital into an hotel in 1954. For a time there
were two comfortable dormitories in addition to the 150 sumptuous
double rooms. The obligation has been gradually whittled away
until today it is limited to providing a maximum of ten pilgrims
who can produce their Compostelas with one free meal a day for
three days.

We had been taken for bona fide guests by the immaculate staff
as we looked around the hotel, and nothing had been too good for
us. The moment we enquired about the free pilgrim dinner, it was
as though we had been fitted with lepers' bells. When we asked one
of the uniformed doormen where the free dinner was served, he
pointed brusquely along the outside wall to the right and turned his
back, muttering '*Por alli.*' 'That way' led us to the hotel garage
where we wandered among the Mercedes and BMWs before finding
an attendant in overalls who led us across a small open courtyard
full of building materials and litter to a side entrance back into the
main body of the hotel. We now entered a very different world from
the suave, glittering one above. The bowels of a hotel are always
interesting, but none more so than those of the Reyes Catolicos.
Dark passages, unpainted, and with exposed pipes running overhead,
damp sawdust and cigarette ends underfoot, led to narrow intersec-
tions where we had to squeeze between overflowing dustbins and
old-fashioned ice-boxes. Cooks and cleaners in dirty aprons stood
smoking in groups and barely moved to let us past, looking down
on forms of life even lower than themselves. A surly cook took us
in charge, handing us each a wooden board on which he slapped
noisily two plates, a knife, fork, spoon and paper napkin. Following
him, we reached a canteen where, feeling like conscripts on our first

day in the army, we watched as noodle soup was slopped messily into our bowls from a cauldron and handed to us with both thumbs, I noticed, well below water level. Next was another giant pot full of potatoes; some of these were piled on our plates, two cold hard-boiled eggs were added and something yellowy-orange was poured over the top. It made a generous mound. We were told to help ourselves to bread and apples, a glass of rosé wine was poured for us and we were off again on another long and winding subterranean journey, balancing our rather precarious loads, until we reached a tatty staff recreation room where round tables were piled among plastic-covered sofas from which the stuffing was escaping. There we were joined by the two young Spanish pilgrims we had seen from the bridge at Furelos, and also five Germans and an Italian girl. No one spoke much, subdued perhaps by the depressing surroundings, and few managed to finish the substantial but relatively cold and unappetizing meal when compared with even the simplest of those we had had along the Way. On leaving we were all shunted back with our dirty trays until we had left them in the kitchen, when we were allowed to leave by the garage again.

Since the hotel is obliged to feed ten pilgrims, it does seem a pity that it cannot be done with better grace. The contrast between life above and below stairs was unnecessarily extreme. Of course those prepared to pay top prices should receive the best treatment and food, but there is no need or excuse for giving charity grudgingly and crudely since it would cost no more to provide a quite different experience and one which would bring great credit on the hotel. Those entitled to receive free meals have worked hard for the privilege and they are the visible expression of the pilgrimage to which Santiago owes its existence. Those who had come by air, sea or road to view the sights of St James's city would − I believe − not object to sharing a small part of their grand dining room with true pilgrims, even if some of them were honourably travel-stained.

Because pilgrims are fed much earlier than the 'real' guests, it was still daylight when we emerged from the garage and climbed up into the square. The sun was setting and its last golden rays were lighting up the façade of El Obradoiro. We sat on a low wall and watched the colours change. From primrose, through saffron and ochre to a rich buttery orange, every shade of red and yellow seemed to mingle on the tangled surface. Suddenly it seemed as though the vault of the sky over the city were itself a great church, the open plaza a wide nave and the ornate west front of the Cathedral, now apparently gilded, had become a giant reredos; the steps to which we had tied our horses only that morning, an altar. It was a moment we will not forget.

AFTERMATH

After it was all over we had some days in hand and so we drove on west into old windswept coastal Galicia, where broad white sandy beaches and towering granite headlands are separated by lengthy inlets or *rías*. Like Cornwall or the west coasts of Ireland and Scotland, the water was cold and the people Celtic. We camped in a pine wood where I could write at a makeshift table, looking out over a wide bay where fishing boats trawled and where, on the shore, Merlin built sand-castles and looked for crabs in rock-pools.

Shellfish were relatively cheap and straight from the sea, especially *percebes* – the delicious, succulent, pink phallic goose barnacles which I have only met along that coast and in Portugal. We sampled other Galician specialities. Padrón peppers, of course; the large ones dangerously hot, the little ones tasting like Japanese seaweed. Prawns, clams and, according to the locals, 'the best mussels in the world'. Tripe and chick-peas, too, served with coarse local wine in little flat cups, and wind-dried salted cod which we had seen suspended from poles in the sun and the spray.

Nearby was a Celtic settlement on a headland, defended on three sides by cliffs and boiling seas, across the isthmus by a series of solid stone walls. The huts were circular, of the same familiar design as those at Cebreiro and on Bodmin Moor, but here they lay at the very edge of what to their inhabitants must once have been the last outpost of the civilized world. Before the ruthless and efficient warfare of the Romans, these Celts must have fought desperate battles, their backs quite literally to a wall of emptiness. To them the Romans were the barbarians: materialistic, dictatorial, ruthless, godless. The defenders may well have been early Christians, too, desperately trying to keep alight the spark of their enlightenment. Just as the Roman church was to do later, the Roman Empire was powerful enough to rewrite history so that any suggestion that those it came to dominate might have had culture, learning and wisdom was extinguished. It was a touching place, sensitively restored and vividly evoking the fragile hold of all Celtic people to the barren lands left them in the far west of Europe.

We also visited the traces of even earlier people: the standing stones, dolmens and cromlechs of prehistoric races. But there the echoes of the past were so faint that, as at Avebury or Stonehenge, there was only a dim aura of long vanished power and great events.

At Padrón the church was closed because, as a notice on the door informed us, a young man had been killed in a car crash and his funeral was due. In Spain, bodies must be buried within 48 hours. The sacristan could not be found, but the parish priest's housekeeper, once I had tracked her down, was helpfulness itself – letting us in, turning on lights and encouraging us to photograph whatever we wished. There was a marvellous 19th-century Santiago Matamoros, riding his white horse in a large glass case over the tangled bodies of three rather effete Moors, who lay on their backs and barely defended themselves. Another case held a figure with scallop-shell, pilgrim staff and floppy hat, whom at first I took to be St James but was sharply corrected by our guide. She explained that this was San Roque. He was a 14th-century hermit and pilgrim from Montpellier, who caught the plague on one of his journeys and was kept alive by a dog which brought him food in the wood where he hid until he was cured. He is easily distinguished from St James as he is always represented coyly lifting his gown to reveal the sore on his leg and accompanied by a faithful hound with a loaf of bread in its mouth. He appears more and is much more popular in France, where he is known as St Roch.

The object which draws tourists and pilgrims to Padrón church is the mooring stone (*o pedrón*) to which the boat which brought St James's body to Spain was said to have been attached. It is hidden beneath the altar, but can be lit up and inspected. A roughly-carved piece of granite like a small gatepost, it has a scoop in the top as though it had once been a simple font. In fact it was originally a Roman altar in the important town which was then called Iria Flavia.

Looking down at this rather unimpressive piece of stone, I felt that as a pilgrim I had come full circle in my quest for St James. The whole story is so exceedingly unlikely and so clearly concocted (at least in parts, possibly in its entirety) to provide a suitable focus for Christian unity in Spain against Islam, that it would be easy to dismiss it all as mere legend. But none of that matters; it is the pilgrimage itself which, from the very moment that the Saint's grave was discovered and identified in A.D. 813 or thereabouts, has created its own momentum, rationale and legacy. Hallowed by millions of feet, its very existence transcends the detail of historical or invented facts upon which it is founded. The myth is what matters, inspiring unnumbered men and women to lead – if only for a time – lives of hardship and self-sacrifice, buoyed up by the spiritual ecstasy which their journey created. St James was very real for all those people, and his example impelled them to superhuman acts of endurance on their travels, courage in their battles with the Moors and creativity in their buildings and works of art. Myth is the corporate conscience of mankind, which teaches us how to live in the world.

While I have a deep respect and affection for Christian myth and tradition, from which I feel neither capable nor desirous of escaping, I believe that the time has come for new myths to develop which are more relevant to our time and to the needs of both our species and our only planet. Going on a pilgrimage helped me to see some things much more clearly. Perhaps that has always been the purpose, whether pilgrims sought expiation of their sins or eternal salvation. Sharing time and space with so many medieval craftsmen endorsed my instinctive belief that life does not have to be modern to be good. There was a contentment which shone out of so many carvings and pictures of a time which is too often dismissed as being one of unmitigated hardship and misery. Today, as confidence in the abilities of science and technology to cure all our ills crumbles, we need models to help us believe that there may be other ways to live in harmony with nature and with ourselves. These peoples, whom some have tended to despise for the simplicity of their lives, produced some of the greatest buildings in history.

Through all the odour of sanctity along the Way of the Saints, I thought I detected a robust scent of earlier trails. While questioning the dogmas which so many seemed to accept, I found that the story of the pilgrimage is itself full of memories of others who questioned accepted thinking and often suffered martyrdom for their heresy. How ironic if the bones – still revered daily by so many beneath the high altar in the cathedral at Santiago de Compostela – really are those of St Priscillian.

The Roman church most effectively suppressed the other early Christian churches such as the Gallican, Celtic and Mozarabic, whose messages differed from its own, but the memories lingered on. Also, of course, the church constantly adapted earlier myths and traditions from pre-Christian times to its own ceremonial. It seems quite likely that there was a route to the west followed by sun worshippers from very earliest times. We had felt the attraction ourselves and had seen the dolmens they had built. Certainly there was a Roman trade route to the far west; there is a feeling of inevitability and rightness all along the Way.

These myths from which so much of Christianity grew still lie deep within our folk memory. Profound beliefs, which are perhaps more like instincts, are buried far down in our communal subconscious. Like seeds which have lain dormant underground for centuries, they are now bursting into bloom all over the world as the greening of our consciousness gives them fertile ground in which to grow.

As we realize that our present myths – whether they be religious, political or scientific – have let us down, and that following them slavishly will not cure and may well destroy the fragile fabric of life on earth, we need to search urgently for new and relevant myths to cling to. Whatever solutions we come up with should not reject the past, believing that new ideas can wholly remove beliefs which lie deep within each of us. That way lies tyranny, as the collapse of Communism has forcefully revealed. No new ideology, however inspired, however timely, can entirely supplant what has gone before. It can, however, revolutionize existing philosophies by adding an ingredient which transforms them and gives them a whole new appropriateness. Just as Christianity introduced love into a cruel world, but otherwise very largely grafted its forms and offices on to the existing Judaic tradition, so could the new green philosophy which permeates so much of the thinking of those genuinely concerned with creating a sustainable world, transform the established religions.

Christianity in all its forms has been slow to recognize these desires among its often only nominal adherents, and even slower to do anything about it. Yet there is an unmistakable longing felt by practising Christians to have their religious beliefs made relevant to the ecological crises facing the modern world. I believe that it would be possible to do this, but that the dogmatic upheaval would be as great as that which split the Protestant church from the church of Rome nearly 500 years ago. The heresy at the heart of that great dispute was the unwillingness of many to accept the dogma of transubstantiation. They simply refused to be party to what they saw as a conspiracy to tell a lie and state that the bread and wine did become flesh and blood when they received them as the sacrament. Many, including my ancestor Anne Askew, died at the stake rather than agree with something they believed to be untrue. Perhaps that Protestant rationality was part of the changing view of the world which has led to materialism causing the global disaster we now fear. Therein would lie a certain irony.

Nevertheless, the greening of Christianity will require that another and possibly harder heresy prevail. This is to deny the special relationship of man with God. If man was made in God's image and given 'dominion over the fish of the sea, and over the fowl of the air, and over the cattle, and over all the earth and over every creeping thing that creepeth upon the earth', he has made a poor job of it and surely that alone forfeits him his special status. If, on the other hand, all creatures were made in God's image, man simply being blessed with an opposed thumb and forefinger and the power of reasoning, then in due humility we should be able to see our way to working with the rest of creation towards a stable world. God's plan would be seen as the welfare of all life, not just the dominion of one species. And since we would share our second-hand divinity with all other living things, the greatest sins would no longer be confined to the murder of our own kind but would include the wanton killing of anything. The destruction of another species would take its rightful place beside genocide as the greatest crime of all. Perhaps it is just as well that they have stopped burning people at the stake for heresy.

Finally there was Finisterre, land's end, Virgil's Ultima Thule; until 1492 the uttermost extremity of the known world. Is it any wonder there should always have been an urge in man to go there and gaze after the setting sun into the unknown? We took our places on a lichen-covered rock on the bleak headland and looked at the silver waves which stretched away to an indistinct horizon. How strange to think that none of those who, for the 500 busiest years of the pilgrimage, reached that point, had any idea that great civilizations lay beyond that ocean. Once Columbus revealed the existence of the New World, much of the steam went out of the pilgrimage. While the Renaissance brought a spate of new and ambitious building, which often included the virtual burying of whole Romanesque structures behind ornate façades, the sardonic worldliness which accompanied all that flamboyance undermined the simple faith of the pilgrim. It is also likely that the Reformation and the spread of new ideas following the invention of printing led many to question the concept of purchasing salvation through penances such as pilgrimage. Nonetheless I believe that Columbus had a lot to do with it, too. While the prime motive for discovery in the New World was and remained economic, there was always a strong and sometimes overpowering religious element. Oddly enough, Christopher Columbus combined both these traits in his own name: Christbearer; Colonizer. And it was his Christian name which was to cause the most trouble. The catastrophic effects of the colonization of people with no resistance to European diseases were horribly compounded by the enthusiasm with which they were forced to clothe themselves, to hide their 'sinful' nakedness and live in unsanitary compounds in order to be proselytized and put to work. Incandescent from the 500 years of religious fervour which fuelled the medieval and Renaissance drive to go on crusades and pilgrimages, the Catholic Church turned with ruthless zeal on the unfortunate inhabitants of the New World. Santiago Matamoros, having chased the last invading Moors out of Spain in that same year, 1492, was now invoked against the Indians who were themselves suffering from the greatest invasion in history. For nearly another 500 deplorable years it strove to subvert, convert, divert the Indians of South America to its philosophy. The only effective resistance was flight, and many of the tribes still retaining their traditional cultures are those who migrated deeper into Amazonas rather than face the relentless slavery which 'civilization' offered them.

In this century the Roman Catholic Church has largely changed its ways and come to work with the people regardless of whether they accept its tenets; many of its priests have been in the forefront of the battles for justice and self-determination. The Second Vatican Council exhorted missionaries to have 'a great respect for the patrimony, language and cultures of the people among whom they work'.

Meanwhile, however – almost unseen and unremarked by the rest of the world – an even more insidious and implacable enemy has appeared, reaching out with especial fervour for those who have so far escaped the contamination of alien and inappropriate Western ideas and attitudes. Spawned in the Deep South and Bible belts of the USA and nourished with the vast sums of money easily taken from a rich and philosophically bankrupt society, they have fed on the single idea that everyone must believe exactly as they do if their souls are to be saved. Apart from the patent nonsense of such a belief to anyone who pauses for a moment to think how many variations of faith and ideology the world has produced, it is a most dangerous attitude when grafted on to missionary zeal. Equipped with unlimited funds to pay for more aeroplanes, radios and comfortable mobile homes, their minions search the world for those who are not already members of one of the major established beliefs as are, of course, the vast majority. Once the victims are found and descended on, they stand little chance of retaining their culture and pride; instead they rapidly lose their identity and become detribalized beggars. It is an all-too-familiar story. Concern for their plight has been my life's great passion, my own Crusade.

Other philosophies and beliefs sit easy with me. So much of my life has been spent travelling among people with such different views of God, spirits and other worlds that I find no difficulty in accepting their views as valid for them and no threat to me. In many ways, the more remote their cosmology is from my own, the easier it is to live with. To accept that rocks, trees, rivers and the beasts and birds of the forests are occupied by spirits which must be honoured echoes my own tribe's belief of only a few generations ago. It also makes good sense in a world rapidly becoming aware of the inter-relationship of all things.

What I cannot tolerate is bigotry, especially when it springs from the essentially free-thinking Protestantism of my own background. Yet apart from Islamic fundamentalism, that is precisely where it appears most manifest and dangerous today. The smug certainty of all fundamentalism repels me, based as it always is on laws and attitudes designed in the name of God by fallible men to cope with conditions far removed from those facing us today. Tragically the blind bigotry of Europeans towards the Amerindian attitude to the environment continues, as much among governments throughout the Americas as among the new breed of Protestant fundamentalist missionaries.

I became aware of a peculiar contradiction in the recognition that the Saint to whose tomb I had just travelled as a pilgrim and the faith which had produced the wonders we had seen along the Way, should have together been responsible for so much evil. I could not regret our pilgrimage; it had been a beautiful, inspiring and fulfilling journey; but what had it taught me? Had my bishop been right when he said that I should not worry, and that by the time I arrived I would know what it was I wanted to say? Well, perhaps he had. I certainly felt a lot clearer in my own mind about many things which before I had found confusing.

As a campaigner for human rights and environmental sense, I am constantly asked if I do not think the whole situation hopeless. 'Hasn't it gone too far?' people say. 'Can we really stop the destruction of the rain-forests and save the tribes who live in them?' Refuting such despair with real conviction has at times been difficult. Sharing one of the world's great spiritual journeys with the shades of so many who went before strengthened my resolve and my belief in the possibilities. Recognizing how fallible man is, how mixed his motives, how much courage and beauty can come when he is inspired, reassured me that, given a new purpose, nothing is impossible. People could and would respond if they came to believe in a new Way.

A pilgrimage is a journey out of time. We had been in the spiritual and cultural company of medieval fellow travellers; we had seen some of the very best of their works and shared the air, the stones and the sights of a landscape which has changed little since they walked it in their millions.

We returned to a world in a turmoil of change and, thanks to the pilgrimage, I saw that change with a more positive and a more passionate hope than I could possibly have had without the experience.

The Superpowers had agreed to start the process of scrapping nuclear weapons, and this time it looked as though they meant it. Communism was crumbling throughout Eastern Europe, and in less than six months the inconceivable was to happen and the Russian Praesidium was to vote to hold free elections. South Africa was moving towards ending apartheid, and the killing of elephants as well as whales was stopping almost everywhere. The green revolution appeared to have developed an irrevocable momentum and, while the world still faced monumental and quite possibly terminal problems, for the first time in my lifetime there was hope.

It was, I realized, time for a new religion, one which could address and satisfy the needs of the new millennium and – almost as though some Gaian force was at work – everything seemed to be conspiring to produce a suitable seedbed for such a fragile flower to grow.

A flood of new books had been published on all sorts of green subjects just in time – it seemed to me – to make it quite impossible to read everything relevant to the fresh ideas our pilgrimage had started me thinking about. Most pertinent were those concerned with the search for a 'theology of ecology'. A leading voice was that of Father Thomas Berry, an American monk who sees us moving into 'a new mythic age' where 'a kind of mutation is taking place in the entire earth – human order'.* He describes ecology as the 'supreme subversive science', confronting and transforming all previously held belief in the ability of industrial society to survive. But he also says that more is needed than just physical change. We must change at a psychic level, too; he tells us, 'the planet Earth and the life communities of the earth are speaking to us through the deepest elements of our nature, through our genetic coding.'

Sean McDonagh, an Irish priest who has spent much of his life with the T'boli people in the Philippines, struck a powerful chord with me in his book *To Care for the Earth*. 'Like tribal people,' he writes, 'we too must once again commune with God in nature.' In a wide-ranging book about the environmental crisis facing us, with particular reference to the Philippines and Ireland, he speaks courageously of 'ecological prayer' and an 'authentic spirituality' emerging from our understanding of the Earth today. He is ready to acknowledge and admire pantheism and pre-Christian religions, thereby showing that no religion, including Christianity, need be defensive and inward-looking. Instead, as a missionary he dares to urge all people to dedicate their lives to caring for the earth.

Meanwhile the sudden popular awareness of the threats to our survival from the destruction of rain-forests and the depletion of the ozone layer led to more uncompromising apocalyptic books with titles like *The End of Nature* (Bill McKibben) and *Hothouse Earth: The Greenhouse Effect and Gaia* (John Gribben) which predicates the flooding of much of the world through rising seas. These and many other books all state unequivocally that the only way we can save ourselves is by undergoing a radical and fundamental change in our attitude towards nature. This is what I mean by a new religion. It may not require the abandonment of the faiths in which we have grown up and learnt to feel secure, but those faiths will have to adapt along the lines being pioneered by Fathers Berry and McDonagh. Hope that this can happen lies in the miraculous spread

The Dream of the Earth, p 132

of a green philosophy which has captured the imagination of so many so fast that suddenly it is affecting everyone's life. It is like a revolution. Potentially its adherents may be just as perverse and autocratic as those belonging to any religious sect, and already there are signs of schisms and sectarianism within the green movement, as there were from the very earliest days of Christianity, but this does not mean that the movement will not grow and produce a new moral code, if not a new religion.

Sir William Golding, the Nobel laureate, in reviewing *Hothouse Earth* wrote: 'There are signs that this revolution in feeling may be at hand. Otherwise the only motive power which will drive our actions will be self-interest, starting in concern, heightened by way of worry to dread: and if the seas really do become a monster, and Gaia an outraged and avenging stepmother, the end will be panic and terror.'*

The greatest barrier to hope since the end of the Second World War has been the fear of a nuclear holocaust. World leaders, farmers, business people and aid workers – like most other inhabitants of the planet – have lived under the threat of learning that they have only four minutes to live. As a result there has seemed no point in planning for the future. Why not, if you are in a position of power, line your pocket at your country's expense? Corruption among politicians is today endemic throughout much of the world, to the extent that many countries have been crippled by it. As recent events have revealed so dramatically, the Communist world has been as guilty as any.

Why should farmers plant for the future if there may not be one? Why protect the fertility of the soil and plant trees that will take 100 years to mature when there may not be a tomorrow? Far more sensible to exploit the land to the maximum, so as to live well in the present.

Volatile stock markets, scandals in the City and loans to both individuals and nations which are unlikely ever to be repaid, are symptoms of a similar nihilism in the world of finance.

When people are starving since their land can no longer feed them because it has been abused, the logical solution should be to reverse the trend by undertaking long-term programmes to rehabilitate it. But if the future holds out no hope anyway, what is the point of directing aid to such slow and difficult processes? Let's feed the refugees from charity, and at least make their deaths less sudden and shocking.

Now all that has changed and there is no longer an excuse for despair. There is no need to spend vast sums on armaments, though

Sunday Times, 28 January 1990

all rapid change brings violence and no one should delude himself that the process will run smoothly. Forces of evil, greed, self-interest, blind nationalism, racial and religious conflict will grasp their opportunities, and it will be well to be strong to combat them.

Today the danger is less that the world may come to an end with an atomic bang than that it may expire with an ecological whimper. Scientists are beginning to recognize and publicize the essential fragility and interdependence of all life on earth, although the more they research life's complexity the more they discover their own ignorance and incapacity to control events. Vast sums are needed urgently to research both the rapidly vanishing natural diversity of the planet and to devise ways of saving it and us. What could be more obvious than that this is the logical destination of all the money saved from the arms race? Just at the very moment when unimaginable resources may be seeking new homes, a need which is even more demonstrably relevant to our security arises. The rich countries of the world need to spend their wealth. Devoting it to undoing the damage we have caused the environment in the past and helping it to recover and prosper will also be the best possible way of helping those countries which otherwise face insoluble problems if all we do is throw money and food at them when our conscience pricks us.

The resources are there, the communication networks are in place, there is a burgeoning universal desire for social justice, the promise of rebirth is held out. All that is needed is the will to do it; a new faith in the future. Like a medieval pilgrim we have our scallop-shell of quiet, our staff of faith, our scrip of joy; the road ahead is prepared and waiting; we believe in the promised salvation. There is even hope.

Appendix 1

Sir Walter Ralegh 1552?–1618
The Passionate Man's Pilgrimage

Give me my scallop-shell of quiet,
My staff of Faith to walk upon,
My scrip of joy, immortal diet,
My bottle of salvation,
My gown of glory, hope's true gage,
And thus I'll take my pilgrimage.

Blood must be my body's balmer,
No other balm will there be given
Whilst my soul, like a white palmer,
Travels to the land of heaven,
Over the silver mountains,
Where spring the nectar fountains;
And there I'll kiss
The bowl of bliss,
And drink my eternal fill
On every milken hill.
My soul will be a-dry before,
But after it will ne'er thirst more.

And by the happy blissful way
More peaceful pilgrims I shall see,
That have shook off their gowns of clay,
And go apparelled fresh like me.
I'll bring them first
To slake their thirst,
And then to taste those nectar suckets,
At the clear wells
Where sweetness dwells,
Drawn up by saints in crystal buckets.

And when our bottles and all we
Are filled with immortality,
Then the holy paths we'll travel
Strewed with rubies thick as gravel,
Ceilings of diamonds, sapphire floors,
High walls of coral, and pearl bowers.

From thence to heaven's bribeless hall,
Where no corrupted voices brawl,
No conscience molten into gold,
Nor forged accusers bought and sold,
No cause deferred, nor vain-spent journey,
For there Christ is the king's attorney,

Who pleads for all without degrees,
And he hath angels, but no fees.

When the grand twelve million jury
Of our sins and sinful fury,
'Gainst our souls black verdicts give,
Christ pleads his death, and then we live.
Be thou my speaker, taintless pleader,
Unblotted lawyer, true proceeder;
Thou movest salvation even for alms,
Not with a bribed lawyer's palms.

And this is my eternal plea
To him that made heaven, earth, and sea:
Seeing my flesh must die so soon,
And want a head to dine next noon,
Just at the stroke, when my veins start and spread,
Set on my soul an everlasting head.
Then am I ready, like a palmer fit,
To tread those blest paths which before I writ.

Appendix 2

The Balad Whych Anne Askewe Made and Sang When She Was in Newgate*

Reprinted from Bale's Account of Anne Askewe

Lyke as the armed knyght
  Appointed to the fielde,
With thys world wyll I fyght,
  And fayth shall be my shielde.

Faythe is that weapon stronge
  Whych wyll not fayle at nede;
My foes therfor amonge
  Therewith wyll I procede.

As it is had in strengthe
  And force of Christes waye,
It wyll prevayle at lengthe
  Though all the devyls saye naye.

Faythe in the fathers olde
  Obtayned rightwysenesse,
Whych make me verye bolde
  To feare no worldes dystresse.

I now rejoyce in hart,
  And hope byd me do so,
For Christ wyll take my part,
  And ease me of my wo.

Thou sayst Lorde, whoso knocke
  To them wylt thu attende;
Undo therfor the locke,
  And thy stronge power sende.

More enmyes now I have,
  Than heeres upon my heed,
Lete them not me deprave,
  But fyght thu in my steed.

On the my care I cast,
  For all their cruel spyght
I sett not by their hast
  For thu art my delyght.

I am not she that lyst
  My anker to lete fall
For everye dryslynge myst;
  My shippe substanciall.

Not oft use I to wryght,
  In prose, nor yet in ryme,
Yet wyll I shewe one syght
  That I sawe in my tyme.

I sawe a ryall trone
  Where Justyce shold have sytt.
But in her stede was one
  Of modye, cruell wytt.

Absorpt was rightwysnesse
  As of the ragynge floude;
Sathan in hys excesse
  Sucte up the gyltelesse bloude.

Then thought I, Jesus Lorde
  Whan thu shalt judge us all,
Harde is it to recorde
  On these men what wyll fall.

Yet Lorde, I the desyre,
  For that they do to me,
Lete them not tast the hyre
  Of their inyquyty.

* Modern sources usually spell her name Anne Askew, although Bale added an 'e'.
However she herself spelt it Ayskough.

Appendix 3

EXTRACTS FROM
THE SONG OF
ROLAND

★

TRANSLATED BY
Dorothy L. Sayers

133

Roland has set Olifant to his lips,
Firmly he holds it and blows it with a will.
High are the mountains, the blast is long and shrill,
Thirty great leagues the sound went echoing.
King Carlon heard it and all who rode with him.
'Lo, now, our men are fighting', quoth the King.
Guènes retorts: 'If any man said this
Except yourself, it were a lie, methinks.'

134

The County Roland with pain and anguish winds
His Olifant, and blows with all his might.
Blood from his mouth comes spurting scarlet-bright
He's burst the veins of his temples outright.
From hand and horn the call goes shrilling high:
King Carlon hears it who through the passes rides,
Duke Naimon hears, and all the French beside.
Quoth Charles: 'I hear the horn of Roland cry!
He'd never sound it but in the thick of fight.'
'There is no battle', Count Ganelon replies;
'You're growing old, your hair is sere and white,
When you speak thus, you're talking like a child.
Full well you know Roland's o'erweening pride;
'Tis strange that God endures him so long time!
Took he not Noples against your orders quite?
The Paynims made a sally from inside,
And there gave battle to Roland the great knight;
So he swilled down the field – a brave device
To keep the bloodstains from coming to your eyes!
For one small hare he'll blow from morn till night;
Now to the Peers he's showing-off in style.

Who dare attack him? No man beneath the sky!
Ride on, ride on! Why loiter here the while?
Our Fathers' land lies distant many a mile.'

135

Count Roland's mouth with running blood is red;
He's burst asunder the temples of his head;
He sounds his horn in anguish and distress.
King Carlon hears, and so do all the French.
Then said the King: 'This horn is long of breath.'
  ''Tis blown', quoth Naimon, 'with all a brave man's strength;
Battle there is, and that I know full well.
He that would stay you is but a traitor fell.
To arms! let sound your battle-cry to heav'n!
Make haste to bring your gallant household help!
You hear how Roland makes desperate lament!'

136

The Emperor Charles lets sound his horns aloft.
The French light down and arm themselves anon
With helm and hauberk and gilded swords girt on;
Goodly their shields, their lances stiff and strong,
Scarlet and white and blue the gonfalons.
Straightway to horse the warrior lords have got;
Swift through the passes they spur and never stop.
Each unto other they speak and make response:
'Might we reach Roland ere he were dead and gone,
We'ld strike good strokes beside him in the throng.'
  What use is that? They have delayed too long.

137

Vespers draws on and shining is the day;
Against the sun glitters their armed array,
Hauberk and helm flash back a mighty blaze,
So many shields their painted flowers display,
Such store of spears with gilded pennons gay!
The Emperor rides right wrathful on his way.
And all the French in anger and dismay;
There is not one but weeps for very rage;
For Roland's sake they're grievously afraid.
The King arrests Count Ganelon straightway;
He's turned him over to the cooks in his train;
The master-cook he calls, Besgun by name:
'Guard me him well, as fits a man so base,
For all my house this villain has betrayed!'
Besgun takes charge, with five-score kitchen knaves.
The best and worst that serve in that estate.

They pluck the beard from off his chin and face,
With four sound thumps each gives him a good baste.
With sticks and faggots they pound him and they paste,
And round his neck they fasten a strong chain,
Right well they chain him like a bear in a cage;
Now on a pack-horse they've hoisted him in shame;
Till Carlon want him 'tis they will keep him safe.

171

Now Roland feels his sight grow dim and weak;
With his last strength he struggles to his feet;
All the red blood has faded from his cheeks.
A grey stone stands before him at his knee:
Ten strokes thereon he strikes, with rage and grief;
It grides, but yet nor breaks nor chips the steel.
'Ah!' cries the Count, 'St Mary succour me!
Alack the day, Durendal, good and keen!
Now I am dying, I cannot fend for thee.
How many battles I've won with you in field!
With you I've conquered so many goodly fiefs
That Carlton holds, the lord with the white beard!
Let none e'er wield you that from the foe would flee –
You that were wielded so long by a good liege!
The like of you blest France shall never see.'

172

Count Roland smites the sardin stone amain.
The steel grides loud, but neither breaks nor bates.
Now when he sees that it will nowise break
Thus to himself he maketh his complaint:
'Ah, Durendal! so bright, so brave, so gay!
How dost thou glitter and shine in the sun's rays!
When Charles was keeping the vales of Moriane,
God by an angel sent to him and ordained
He should bestow thee on some count-capitayne.
On me he girt thee, the noble Charlemayn.
With this I won him Anjou and all Bretayn,
With this I won him Poitou, and conquered Maine;
With this I won him Normandy's fair terrain,
And with it won Provence and Acquitaine,
And Lombardy and all the land Romayne,
Bavaria too, and the whole Flemish state,
And Burgundy and all Apulia gained;
Constantinople in the King's hand I laid;
In Saxony he speaks and is obeyed;
With this I won Scotland, [Ireland and Wales,]*

*the text is corrupt; but either Ireland or Wales is certainly intended,
and possibly both [*Translator*].

And England, where he set up his domain;
What lands and countries I've conquered by its aid,
For Charles to keep whose beard is white as may!
Now am I grieved and troubled for my blade;
Should Paynims get it, 'twere worse than all death's pains.
Dear God forbid it should put France to shame!'

174

Now Roland feels death press upon him hard;
It's creeping down from his head to his heart.
Under a pine-tree he hastens him apart,
There stretches him face down on the green grass,
And lays beneath him his sword and Olifant.
He's turned his head to where the Paynims are,
And this he doth for the French and for Charles,
Since fain is he that they should say, brave heart,
That he has died a conquerer at the last.
He beats his breast full many a time and fast,
Gives, with his glove, his sins into God's charge.

176

The County Roland lay down beneath a pine;
To land of Spain he's turned him as he lies,
And many things begins to call to mind:
All the broad lands he conquered in his time,
And fairest France, and the men of his line,
And Charles his lord, who bred him from a child;
He cannot help but weep for them and sigh.
Yet of himself he is mindful betimes;
He beats his breast and on God's mercy cries:
'Father most true, in whom there is no lie,
Who didst from death St Lazarus make to rise,
And bring out Daniel safe from the lions' might,
Save Thou my soul from danger and despite
Of all the sins I did in all my life.'

His right-hand glove he's tendered unto Christ,
And from his hand Gabriel accepts the sign.*
Straightway his head upon his arm declines;
With folded hands he makes an end and dies.
God sent to him His Angel Cherubine,**
And great St Michael of Peril-by-the-Tide;
St Gabriel too was with them at his side;
The County's soul they bear to Paradise.

*the sign – The glove is offered and accepted in token of Roland's
surrender to God of the life which he holds as a fief from Him.
Compare Marsilion's surrender to Baligant of the fief of Spain (LL.
2830–2838).
**Cherubine – 'Cherubin' seems to be used by the poet as the name
of an individual angel.

Appendix 4

THE

PILGRIM TO COMPOSTELLA:

BEING

THE LEGEND OF A COCK AND A HEN,

TO THE HONOUR AND GLORY OF

SANTIAGO.

Robert Southey

The Legend.

PART I.

Once on a time three Pilgrims true,
Being Father and Mother and Son,
For pure devotion to the Saint,
This pilgrimage begun.

Their names, little friends, I am sorry to say,
In none of my books can I find;
But the son, if you please, we'll call Pierre,
What the parents were call'd, never mind.

From France they came, in which fair land
They were people of good renown;
And they took up their lodging one night on the way
In La Calzada town.

Now, if poor Pilgrims they had been,
And had lodged in the Hospice instead of the Inn,
My good little women and men,
Why then you never would have heard,
This tale of the Cock and the Hen.

For the Innkeepers they had a daughter,
Sad to say, who was just such another,
As Potiphar's daughter, I think, would have been
If she follow'd the ways of her mother.

This wicked woman to our Pierre
Behaved like Potiphar's wife;

And, because she fail'd to win his love,
She resolved to take his life.

So she pack'd up a silver cup
In his wallet privily;
And then, as soon as they were gone,
She raised a hue and cry.

The Pilgrims were overtaken,
The people gather'd round,
Their wallets were search'd, and in Pierre's
The silver cup was found.

They dragg'd him before the Alcayde;
A hasty Judge was he,
'The theft,' he said, 'was plain and proved,
And hang'd the thief must be.'
So to the gallows our poor Pierre
Was hurried instantly.

If I should now relate
The piteous lamentation,
Which for their son these parents made,
My little friends, I am afraid
You'd weep at the relation.

But Pierre in Santiago still
His constant faith profess'd;
When to the gallows he was led,
''Twas a short way to Heaven,' he said,
'Though not the pleasantest.'

And from their pilgrimage he charged
His parents not to cease,
Saying that unless they promised this,
He could not be hang'd in peace.

They promised it with heavy hearts;
Pierre then, therewith content,
Was hang'd: and they upon their way
To Compostella went.

PART II.

Four weeks they travell'd painfully,
They paid their vows, and then
To La Calzada's fatal town
Did they come back again.

The Mother would not be withheld,
But go she must to see

Where her poor Pierre was left to hang
Upon the gallows tree.

Oh tale most marvellous to hear,
Most marvellous to tell!
Eight weeks had he been hanging there,
And yet was alive and well!

'Mother,' said he, 'I am glad you're return'd.
It is time I should now be released:
Though I cannot complain that I'm tired,
And my neck does not ache in the least.

'The Sun has not scorch'd me by day,
The Moon has not chill'd me by night;
And the winds have but help'd me to swing,
As if in a dream of delight.

'Go you to the Alcayde,
That hasty Judge unjust,
Tell him Santiago has saved me,
And take me down he must!'

Now, you must know the Alcayde,
Not thinking himself a great sinner,
Just then at table had sate down,
About to begin his dinner.

His knife was raised to carve,
The dish before him then;
Two roasted fowls were laid therein,
That very morning they had been
A Cock and his faithful Hen.

In came the Mother wild with joy;
'A miracle!' she cried;
But that most hasty Judge unjust
Repell'd her in his pride.

'Think not,' quoth he, 'to tales like this
That I should give belief!
Santiago never would bestow
His miracles, full well I know,
On a Frenchman and a thief.'

And pointing to the Fowls, o'er which
He held his ready knife,
'As easily might I believe
These birds should come to life!'

The good Saint would not let him thus
The Mother's true tale withstand;

So up rose the Fowls in the dish,
And down dropt the knife from his hand.

The Cock would have crow'd if he could;
To cackle the Hen had a wish;
And they both slipt about in the gravy
Before they got out of the dish.

Cluck! cluck! cried the Hen right merrily then,
The Cock his clarion blew,
Full glad was he to hear again
His own cock-a-doo-del-doo!

PART III.

'A miracle!' a miracle!'
The people shouted, as they might well,
When the news went through the town;
And every child and woman and man
Took up the cry, and away they ran
To see Pierre taken down.

They made a famous procession;
My good little women and men,
Such a sight was never seen before,
And I think will never again.

Santiago's Image, large as life,
Went first with banners and drum and fife;
And next, as was most meet,
The twice-born Cock and Hen were borne
Along the thronging street.

Perch'd on a cross-pole hoisted high,
They were raised in sight of the crowd;
And, when the people set up a cry,
The Hen she cluck'd in sympathy,
And the Cock he crow'd aloud.

And because they very well knew for why
They were carried in such solemnity,
And saw the Saint and his banners before 'em,
They behaved with the greatest propriety,
And most correct decorum.

The Knife, which had cut off their heads that morn,
Still red with their innocent blood, was borne,
The scullion boy he carried it;
And the Skewers also made a part of the show,
With which they were truss'd for the spit.

The Cook in triumph bore the Spit
As high as he was able;
And the Dish was display'd wherein they were laid
When they had been served at table.

With eager faith the crowd prest round;
There was a scramble of women and men
For who should dip a finger-tip
In the blessed Gravy then.

Next went the Alcayde, beating his breast,
Crying aloud like a man distrest,
And amazed at the loss of his dinner,
'Santiago, Santiago!
Have mercy on me a sinner!'

And lifting oftentimes his hands
Towards the Cock and Hen,
'*Orate pro nobis!*' devoutly he cried,
And as devoutly the people replied,
Whenever he said it, 'Amen!'

The Father and Mother were last in the train;
Rejoicingly they came,
And extoll'd, with tears of gratitude,
Santiago's glorious name.

So, with all honours that might be,
They gently unhang'd Pierre;
No hurt or harm had he sustain'd,
But, to make the wonder clear,
A deep black halter-mark remain'd
Just under his left ear.

Appendix 5

St. Francis of Assisi (1182–1226)

The Canticle of Brother Sun

Most high, all powerful, all good Lord!
All praise is yours, all glory, all honour and blessing.
To you, alone, Most High, do they belong.
No mortal lips are worthy
To pronounce your name.
All praise be yours, my Lord, through all that you have made,
And first my Lord Brother Sun,
Who brings the day; and light you give to us through him.
How beautiful is he, how radiant in all his splendour!
Of you, most high, he bears the likeness.
All praise be yours, my Lord, through Sister Moon and Stars;
In the heavens you have made them, bright
And precious and fair.
All praise be Yours, my Lord, through Brothers Wind and Air,
And fair and stormy, all the weather's moods,
By which You cherish all that You have made.
All praise be Yours, my Lord, through the Sister Water,
So useful, lowly, precious and pure.
All praise be Yours, my Lord, through Brother Fire,
Through whom you brighten up the night.
How beautiful he is, how gay! Full of power and strength.
All praise be yours, my Lord, through Sister Earth, my mother
Who feeds us in her sovereignty and produces
Various fruits with coloured flowers and herbs.

SPANISH PILGRIMAGE

Itinerary

Day and Date (1989)		From To	Distance (total) in kms.	Hours (total)
1	Wed 9 August	Roncesvalles – Larrasoaña	26	6
2	Thurs 10 ''	Larrasoaña – Cizur Menor	25 (51)	5 (11)
3	Fri 11 ''	Cizur Menor – Estella	44 (95)	8¼ (19¼)
4	Sat 12 ''	Rest Day		
5	Sun 13 ''	Estella – Viana	34 (129)	7¾ (27)
6	Mon 14 ''	Viana – Nájera	35 (164)	8 (35)
7	Tue 15 ''	Nájera – Sto Domingo	24 (188)	5 (40)
8	Wed 16 ''	Rest Day		
9	Thurs 17 ''	Sto Domingo – Villafranca	34 (222)	6 (46)
10	Fri 18 ''	Villafranca – Tárdajos	46 (268)	9 (55)
11	Sat 19 ''	Tárdajos – Hontanas	21 (289)	2¾ (57¾)
12	Sun 20 ''	Hontanas – Frómista	37 (326)	8 (65¾)
13	Mon 21 ''	Frómista – Moratinos	46 (372)	6¾ (72½)
14	Tue 22 ''	Moratinos – Mansilla de las Mulas	46 (418)	7½ (80)
15	Wed 23 ''	Mansilla – León	17 (435)	3 (83)
16	Thurs 24 ''	Rest Day		
17	Fri 25 ''	León – Orbigo	34 (469)	5 (88)
18	Sat 26 ''	Orbigo – Rabanal	41 (510)	6 (94)
19	Sun 27 ''	Rabanal – Cacabelos	42 (552)	8½ (102½)
20	Mon 28 ''	Cacabelos – Cebreiro	40 (592)	8½ (111)
21	Tue 29 ''	Cebreiro – Samos	32 (624)	5½ (116½)
22	Wed 30 ''	Samos – Portomarín	33 (657)	7 (123½)
23	Thurs 31 ''	Portomarín – Palas do Rei	27 (684)	4 (127½)
24	Fri 1 Sept	Palas do Rei – Arzúa	29 (713)	6 (133½)
25	Sat 2 ''	Arzúa – Monxoi	34 (747)	5 (138½)
26	Sun 3 ''	Monxoi – Santiago	10 (757)	1½ (140)

This represents an average speed of 5.4 kms per hour (3.4 mph) on 23 riding days.

BIBLIOGRAPHY

ALVEY, ADA, *The Search of St James*, Redruth, Cornish Publications 1989.

BERRY, THOMAS, *The Dream of the Earth*, San Francisco, Sierra Club Books 1988.

BORROW, GEORGE, *The Bible in Spain*, London, John Murray 1907.

BRAULT, GERARD J., *The Song of Roland*, Penn State University Press 1978.

CHADWICK, HENRY, *Priscillian of Avila*, Oxford 1976.

CHATWIN, BRUCE, *What Am I Doing Here?*, London, Cape 1988.

CHAUCER, G., *The Canterbury Tales*.

Codex Calixtinus, Guia trads. Millar Bravo Lozano. Sahagún, Centro Estrdios 1989.

COX, IAN (ed)., *The Scallop*, London, Shell 1957.

DAVIES, HORTON & Marie-Helène, *Holy Days and Holidays*, Associated University Press, London 1982.

DENNETT, LAURIE, *A Hug for the Apostle*, Toronto, Macmillan 1987.

ELIAS VALINA SAMPEDRO, *El Camino de Santiago: Guia del Peregrino*, León, Everest 1985.

FINUCANE, RONALD C., *Miracles & Pilgrims*, London, J. M. Dent 1977.

FLANAGAN, SABINA, *Hildegard de Bingen: A Visionary Life*, Routledge, London, 1989

FLETCHER, RICHARD, *Saint James's Catapult*, O.U.P. 1984.

_____ *The Quest for El Cid*, Hutchinson 1989.

FORD, RICHARD, *A Handbook for Travellers in Spain*, London, Centaur Press 1966.

FOXE, JOHN, *The Acts and Monuments*.

FURNIVALL, F. J., *The Stacions of Rome and the Pilgrims Sea Voyage*, London 1867.

HALL, D. J., *English Medieval Pilgrimage*, Kegan Paul, London 1966.

HARTLEY, G. G., *The Story of Santiago de Compostela*, New York 1912.

HEATH, SIDNEY, *Pilgrim Life in the Middle Ages*, London 1911.

HELL, VERA and HELLMUT, *The Great Pilgrimage of the Middle Ages*, Barrie & Rockliff, London 1966.

JUSSERAND, J. J., *English Wayfaring Life in the Middle Ages*. London: Unwin, 1925

KING, GEORGIANA GODDARD, *The Way of Saint James*, Putnam, New York, 1920

LANGLAND, W., *Piers Plowman*, Trans. J. E. Goodridge, Penguin, London, 1959

LANGTON, ROBERT, *The Pilgrimage of Robert Langton*, Harvard U.P., 1924.

LAYTON, T. A., *The Way of St James*, George Allen & Unwin, London 1976.

LOVELOCK, J. E., *Gaia*, O.U.P., 1979.

MCDONAGH, SEAN, *To Care for the Earth*, Geoffrey Chapman, London 1988.

MICHELIN. *Green Guide to Spain*.

MITCHENER, JAMES, *Iberica*, London, Secker & Warburg 1968.

MORRIS, JAN, *Spain*, Barrie and Jenkins, London, 1988.

MULLINS, EDWIN, *The Pilgrimage to Santiago*, Secker & Warburg, London 1974

NEILLANDS, ROB, *The Road to Compostela*, Ashbourne, Moorland 1985.

ROBERTSON, IAN, *Blue Guide: Spain*, London, A. & C. Black 1989.

SALZMAN, L. F., *English Life in the Middle Ages*, O.U.P., London, 1926

SAVAGE, KATHERINE, *The History of World Religions*, London, Bodley Head 1966.

SOUTHEY, ROBERT, *Poetical Works*, London 1838.

STARKIE, WALTER, *The Road to Santiago*, John Murray, London 1951.

SUMPTION, JONATHAN, *Pilgrimage: An Image of Mediaeval Religion*, London, Faber & Faber 1975.

TATE, BRIAN & MARCUS, *The Pilgrim Route to Santiago*, Oxford, Phaidon 1987.

VERON, GEORGES et al., *Le Chemin de Saint Jacques de Compostelle*, Éditions Randonnées Pyrénéennes 1986.

WAY, WILLIAM, *The Itineraries of William Way, Fellow of Eton College, to Jerusalem, A.D. 1458 and A.D. 1462; and to St James of Compostela, A.D. 1456*, Roxburghe Club, London, 1857.

WYLLY, Col. H. C., *XVth (The King's) Hussars 1759–1913*, London, Caxton 1914.

Index

Part of the royalties from this book will go to the Confraternity of St James. In particular I would like to thank the Chairperson Patricia Quaife, who was kind enough to read the text although of course responsibility for any errors is mine.

R H-T

The Confraternity of St James

President: H. E. The Spanish Ambassador

The Confraternity of St James was founded in 1983 to promote the pilgrim route to Santiago de Compostela and to bring together people interested in its history, art, architecture, music, religions and traditions. It is a non-denominational registered charity which organizes a range of activities for its members, including research into the history of the pilgrimage from Britain. Its pilgrim guides to the routes in France and Spain provide practical information for the independent traveller. Other European countries have societies similar to the Confraternity and a number of international events are arranged.

One of its projects, in conjunction with a sister association in Spain, is the restoration of the historic parish house in an isolated village on the pilgrim road as a hostel for walkers, cyclists and riders. The Rabanal Hostel Appeal Fund is aiming to raise £50,000 for the rebuilding work and for future maintenance.

The Hon. Secretary, Marion Marples, will be pleased to send you further details of the appeal and the Confraternity's activities, publications and membership. Her address is:

45 Dolben Street
London
SE1 0UQ